D0481453

STEALING
DEMOCRACY

★　★　★　★　★　★　★

STEALING

DEMOCRACY

★ ★ ★ ★ ★ ★ ★ ★ ★ ★ ★ ★

THE NEW POLITICS
OF VOTER SUPPRESSION

★ ★ ★ ★ ★ ★ ★ ★ ★ ★ ★ ★

SPENCER OVERTON

W. W. NORTON & COMPANY

NEW YORK   LONDON

Copyright © 2006 by Spencer Overton

All rights reserved
Printed in the United States of America
First Edition

For information about permission to reproduce selections from this
book, write to Permissions, W. W. Norton & Company, Inc., 500 Fifth
Avenue, New York, NY 10110

Manufacturing by The Maple-Vail Book Manufacturing Group
Book design by JAM Design
Production manager: Andrew Marasia

Library of Congress Cataloguing-in-Publication Data
Overton, Spencer,
Stealing democracy : the new politics of voter suppression /
Spencer Overton,
p. cm.
Includes bibliographical references and index.
ISBN-13: 978-0-393-06159-8 (hardcover)
ISBN-10: 0-393-06159-0 (hardcover)
1. Elections—United States. 2. Voting—United States.
3. Representative government and representation—United States.
4. Democracy—United States. 5. United States—Politics and
government. I. Title.
JK1976.O94 2006
324.6'5—dc22
2006002026

W. W. Norton & Company, Inc., 500 Fifth Avenue, New York, N.Y. 10110
www.wwnorton.com

W. W. Norton & Company, Ltd., Castle House, 75/76 Wells Street, London W1T 3QT

1 2 3 4 5 6 7 8 9 0

This book is dedicated to my parents,

STERLING AND MILDRED OVERTON.

My appreciation of their selflessness in

raising me grows deeper each day.

CONTENTS

STEALING
DEMOCRACY

★   ★   ★   ★   ★   ★   ★

INTRODUCTION

THE MATRIX

In the end the Party would announce that two and two
made five, and you would have to believe it.

—George Orwell, *Nineteen Eighty-Four*

"I was amazed. . . . I wasn't prepared for it to be a good
movie," Rick Clerici, a Massachusetts therapist, told the
Boston Herald newspaper. "*The Matrix* reminded me of Huxley
and Orwell in that vision of control over the larger reality. . . . We
have some measure of control in our tiny personal lives but the
larger reality is manipulated by far greater forces."

Clerici was not alone. In 1999, the movie took in more than $450
million worldwide, making it a huge hit for Warner Bros. Studios.

In *The Matrix*, thirty-something Thomas Anderson (Keanu
Reeves) plods through life as a software programmer at the mega-
corporation Metacortex. Anderson often arrives late to his cubicle,
weary from a late night of moonlighting as a computer hacker who
operates under the alias "Neo."

Neo intuitively suspects that something is amiss in the world. He
can't put a finger on what's wrong, but the search for answers
consumes him. Neo starts receiving cryptic messages via computer

and telephone about "the Matrix" from a mysterious voice who calls himself Morpheus—played by Laurence Fishburne. As the story unfolds, Neo is guided to Morpheus.

In response to Neo's longing to learn the meaning of the Matrix, Morpheus explains:

> It's that feeling you have had all your life. That feeling that some-thing was wrong with the world. You don't know what it is but it's there, like a splinter in your mind, driving you mad, driving you to me. But what is it? . . . The Matrix is everywhere, it's all around us, here even in this room. You can see it out your window, or on your television. You feel it when you go to work, or go to church or pay your taxes. It is the world that has been pulled over your eyes to blind you from the truth.

Morpheus reveals that the date is approximately 2199, and that the 1999 life that Neo thought was reality is actually a computer-generated virtual experience. Most human beings, Morpheus reveals, are physically warehoused in stacks of gelatin cocoons filled with fluid and tended to by man-made artificial intelligence. The machines hard-wire the humans with a program to create what the humans perceive as their lives. This dreamscape is much more comfortable than reality. People in the Matrix casually dine on vir-tual steak, for example, while Morpheus and his band of rebels sur-vive on bowls of slop that resembles cottage cheese. Morpheus explains that the villain is not a single physical machine or entity, but instead "a neural-interactive simulation that we call the Matrix." The simulation placates most human minds into unques-tioning acceptance of their captivity, while the parasitic machines drain energy from the encapsulated human bodies.

Morpheus leads a band of underground rebels and nurtures Neo's gifts to remake the Matrix and liberate humankind from its own creation. "[C]ontrol the Matrix," Morpheus explains to Neo, "and you control the future."

The *Matrix's* script drew from biblical texts, higher-level math, classic literature such as *Alice in Wonderland*, and Greek mythology. While the popularity of the movie arose in part from its action scenes, the theme of questioning invisible systems that control our lives also spoke to contemporary audiences.

"Many people these days are questioning the reality they have been socially conditioned to perceive," John Bates, a forty-three-year-old computer consultant who saw the film six times, told the *Herald*. The theme of questioning the systems that organize our "reality" also spoke to the actor who played Neo. "It starts with my character asking, 'What is the Matrix?' and from there you're asking, 'What is reality? What is around me?' " said Keanu Reeves. "The film also introduces themes of choice and what happens when you make choices. You can either learn about reality . . . or you can go on living in ignorance."

"The idea of *The Matrix* is that it's very easy to live an unexamined life," *Matrix* co-director Larry Wachowski explained. "It's not just computers; it's about anything you allow to think for you, systems of thought."

VIRTUAL DEMOCRACY

Most people have a relatively simple understanding of American democracy. Each person has a right called a "vote." A person casts the vote for a candidate. The candidates who receive the most votes win and make laws. Candidates win by supporting popular policies. "Free" citizens thus govern themselves.

But contrary to conventional perception, American democracy is not an organic, grassroots phenomenon that mirrors society's pref-

erences. In reality, the will of the people is channeled by a prede-
termined matrix of thousands of election regulations and practices
that most people accept as natural: the location of election-district
boundaries, voter-registration deadlines, and the number of voting
machines at a busy polling place. This structure of election rules,
practices, and decisions filters out certain citizens from voting and
organizes the electorate. There is no "right" to vote outside of the
terms, conditions, hurdles, and boundaries set by the matrix.

Although most people are oblivious to the matrix, it has very real
consequences. In our closely divided political environment, even an
obscure election rule in a single state can determine who sits in the
White House or which party controls Congress. Collectively, the
various rules and practices result in a class of politicians that control
various aspects of Americans' lives, such as the number of students
in a second-grade classroom in Detroit, the level of mercury in the
air we breathe, and the matter of whether a student in the Army
Reserve will sleep in his University of Iowa dormitory or in a bar-
racks in Baghdad, Iraq.[1] And because the United States is a military
and financial superpower, the matrix affects not just Americans but
also hundreds of millions of humans around the globe.

The matrix is *not* a grand conspiracy orchestrated by a single mas-
termind. Instead, it is a collection of ever-changing rules and practices employed by various partisans and bureaucrats that converge to
shape who goes to the polls and which votes are counted. Although
no single individual is in control, some enjoy more influence, such as
legislators who draft election law, secretaries of state, election commissioners, county election boards, poll challengers, and poll workers. These individuals justify their actions using seemingly innocuous
terms like "budgetary constraints," "states' rights," "administrative
convenience," or "prevention of fraud." But whatever the stated reason, their decisions often exclude particular voters, enhance the
power of certain politicians, and advance specific policy preferences.

This is a critical moment for American democracy. Evolved technology—which can process each voter's address, race, gender, political affiliation, and likelihood of voting—enhances politicians' ability to tailor election-district boundaries to include voters who favor them, purge selected voters from registration rolls, and manipulate the matrix in other ways. Cash-strapped municipalities and states hesitate to spend limited tax dollars on better voting machines or more staffing at polls, while better-heeled counties have the resources to ensure that every one of their votes gets counted. An influx of immigrant populations from Latin America and Asia threatens the political status quo in certain communities across the nation, but bilingual ballots and translators are often not provided. Efforts by the United States to promote democracy abroad are compromised by the fact that our political process falls short at home. At this pivotal juncture we should accept the matrix passively, but question it.

There is no way to eliminate the matrix completely. Voting requires ground rules. But we can remake the matrix so that it more fairly empowers all voters rather than simply privileging the insiders who know how to manipulate it. America's founders divided government power among executive, legislative, and judicial branches in order to prevent abuses. By manipulating election rules and tolerating election flaws, however, politicians weaken the most effective check on government abuse—the people.

Rather than obscure the matrix with the soundbites of self-interested political insiders or the dry jargon of academic elites, this book uses real-life stories to show how the matrix affects all Americans.

Chapter 1 shows how the fox too often guards the henhouse in American politics. Incumbent politicians draw the boundaries of their own election districts to ensure that they cannot lose an election, and partisan secretaries of state feign neutrality in administering elections but issue decisions that too often follow the party line.

Chapter 2 explains how local control allows for unequal and under-funded elections, as well as partisan manipulation that excludes voters. Chapter 3 grapples with the provocative question of whether race still matters in twenty-first-century American politics. Chapter 4 explains the continued need for provisions of the federal Voting Rights Act that ensure that changes to voting rules made by state and local politicians are not discriminatory. In response to English-only advocates' attacks on bilingual ballots, chapter 5 explains the need to make voting accessible to all citizens. Chapter 6 describes an emerging antifraud movement that proposes measures such as photo-ID requirements, which threaten to exclude many more legitimate voters than fraudulent ones. The book concludes by focusing on a few average Americans who—despite the demands of business and family—make time to work on democratic reforms in their community.

Americans are not inevitably destined to a fate in which a narrow class of political elites controls the matrix. Change is possible. This book is a road map for bringing the power of the vote back into our hands.[2]

CHAPTER ONE

HOW TO RIG ELECTIONS

In March 2001, Republicans held a five-seat majority in the U.S. House of Representatives. Because of its massive size, California would account for fifty-three seats in the House—or almost one of every eight seats. Political junkies across the nation eagerly waited to see whether California—where Democrats controlled the state legislature—would redraw district boundaries to replace three Republican incumbents with Democrats and steal the U.S. House from the Republicans.

The task of drafting California's new district boundaries did not fall to officeholders or their staffers, but rather to a chain-smoking, rumpled political consultant hired by Democrats. Fifty-three-year-old Michael Berman was a principal partner of BAD Campaigns, a firm known for running expensive campaigns featuring hard-hitting television spots and direct mail for many of California's most powerful Democrats. But during redistricting season, the publicity-shy Berman toiled alone in his Beverly Hills office on Wilshire Boulevard, where various maps cluttered his walls. Berman played an instrumental role in mapping the districts following the 1970, 1980, and 1990 census counts. "He understands the stuff. He understands all the history of the districts," said Phil Burton, a former California state legislator who worked with Berman to pick up six additional congressional seats for Democrats following the 1980 census. Friends described Berman as "brilliant," "demanding," and "fingernail-biting."

The way in which politicians and consultants like Michael Berman decide to group voters can determine political winners and losers. By analogy, think of a classroom of twenty-five high school juniors, consisting of fifteen "math nerds" and ten popular "cool kids" with little interest in academics. The teacher asks the math nerds to divide the class into five study groups. The math nerds might segregate themselves into three all-nerd calculus study groups and also create two cool-kid cliques that gossip about Friday night's house party. If the nerds want to curb chitchat among the cool kids, they might create five less-rigorous geometry study groups, each consisting of three nerds and two cool kids. In similar fashion, politicians draw electoral boundaries to manipulate the composition of Republican or Democratic voters in each district. But instead of doctoring the types of conversations among teenagers, politicians can group voters so that incumbents will almost always beat challenger candidates, or so that candidates from one party—such as Democrats—are almost guaranteed to win in most of the districts.

Imagine, for example, that Democratic state legislators control the redistricting process. In the last election, a Republican incumbent earned 51 percent of the vote to beat a Democratic challenger in the First District. In crafting the new boundaries of the First District, Democratic line-drawers might subtract fifteen largely Republican suburban precincts from the west side of the First District and add fifteen largely Democratic urban precincts to the east side of the district. The new, "gerrymandered" First District reduces the number of voters likely to cast a ballot for the First District's Republican incumbent from 51 percent to 45 percent, greatly enhancing the chances that a Democratic challenger will win the next election.

Every ten years following the U.S. Census, all of the states must revise their U.S. House boundaries so that each district within the state has the same number of people and meets one person/one vote requirements. A similar process is undertaken to revise the state legislative districts. In California and in thirty-five other states, politicians in state legislatures redraw their own districting maps as well as the map for the U.S. House members.[1]

In previous rounds of redistricting, Michael Berman worked with California politicians to craft a map that ensured their own reelections and advanced Democratic Party interests. Following the 1980 census, Berman drew districts that favored sitting politicians of both parties while expanding the Democrats' edge so that the party picked up an additional six congressional seats in 1982. Among the Democratic freshmen who won election to Congress that year was the mapmaker's older brother, Howard Berman.

In the early 1990s, California's Democratic congressional delegation paid Michael Berman $250,000 to devise a plan that maximized Democratic seats. Democratic Assemblyman Willie Brown (who later became mayor of San Francisco) was a key player in promoting the new map, and he told the *Los Angeles Times*, "[Redistricting] may appear to be self-serving for [lawmakers], it may very well be self-serving, but nevertheless it's no different than school finance, no different than mental health, no different than anything else, except the member happens to be directly involved." Republican Governor Pete Wilson vetoed the plan, and the redistricting process went to the California Supreme Court. The court appointed three retired judges, who created more competitive districts that were used for the next decade.

In 2001, the California state legislature would draw three new maps that would assign a total of 173 districts: fifty-three U.S. House seats, forty State Senate seats, and eighty State Assembly seats. Democrats—who held 62 percent of California's U.S. House seats and a slightly higher percentage of State Senate and State

Assembly seats—effectively controlled the process and hired Berman to draw the new U.S. House and State Senate maps. (Another consultant would draft the State Assembly map with Berman's input.) State Democrats paid Berman $1.36 million to draw the State Senate districts, and incumbent Democratic members of Congress collectively paid him about $600,000 ($20,000 each) to draw the U.S. House map. "Twenty thousand is nothing to keep your seat," Democratic Congresswoman Loretta Sanchez told the *Orange County Register.* "I spend $2 million [campaigning] every election. If my colleagues are smart, they'll pay their $20,000, and Michael will draw the district they can win in. Those who have refused to pay? God help them."

Berman had a few options. The mapmaker could try to take over a few Republican districts. But doing so would require draining Democratic voters from relatively safe Democratic districts and putting such districts at risk to Republican challengers. A second factor counseled restraint: California state law stipulated that any redistricting map that did not receive approval from two-thirds of the state legislature could be challenged by the voters in a referendum. At least a few Republican legislators needed to support the plan to ensure that voters would not block it and divert redistricting to judges who might draw more competitive districts.

"If a redistricting plan goes to court, both parties lose control. And once it goes to court, you never know what the outcome will be," said Herb Alexander, an emeritus professor of political science at the University of Southern California. "It also lengthens the process and you don't know what's going to happen in the next months, or in time for the next election."

Elected officials from both parties seemed ready to deal. "Not through any altruism on my part or the leadership of the party in general, but purely through self-interest I believe a reasonable and fair redistricting is the way to go," Democratic Assemblyman John Longville, chair of the redistricting committee in the State

Assembly, told the *San Diego Union-Tribune* in May 2001. Republican Assemblyman Roy Ashburn, vice chair of the redistricting committee, told the newspaper, "I think it's very possible to think we can achieve a bipartisan redistricting. . . . It takes openness and willingness to compromise."

Throughout the spring and summer, Berman toyed with a variety of possible maps. "The computer is almost irrelevant for Michael," explained Professor Bruce Cain, director of the Institute of Governmental Studies at the University of California, Berkeley. "Berman thinks, dreams and breathes the lines," wrote the *Orange County Register*. "He has read reams of census data months in advance—line after line of numbers. On many days, he sits in his office alone, moving population numbers, voting-tendency analyses and political boundaries around in his head."

In September 2001, California lawmakers unveiled the new maps for the U.S. House, State Senate, and State Assembly. In order to reach the two-thirds vote needed to immunize them from referendum challenge, Democrats struck a deal with Republicans. The new maps would protect almost all Republican and Democratic incumbents. Democrats would maintain their majority, but Republicans would not lose any additional seats. Thus, the existing balance of seats in the State Assembly and State Senate would remain unchanged. Democrats would pick up the one additional U.S. House seat that California obtained due to population growth; thus, the congressional delegation would be thirty-three Democrats to twenty Republicans.

"The congressional lines . . . are part of a private deal cut by Karl Rove [President Bush's chief political adviser] and the Democrats," Republican redistricting expert Tony Quinn told the *Copley News Service*. According to the *Los Angeles Times*, the Bush White House pushed to maintain the status quo, even though it favored Democrats, in order to preserve Republican control of Congress.

Thanks to Berman's new plan, incumbents and parties not only would hang on to their existing seats but also would be safer from discontented voters. For example, Democratic U.S. House members Lois Capps, Susan Davis, Jane Harman, Mike Honda, and Adam Schiff all survived closely contested races in 2000, but they would enjoy relatively safe districts in 2002. In 2000, Democrat Michael Case made a strong but ultimately unsuccessful run against Republican U.S. House incumbent Elton Gallegly in a district where registered Democrats accounted for 40 percent of the voters, and registered Republicans 39 percent. But Case decided not to make another run in 2002 after redistricting inflated registered Republicans to 46 percent and deflated registered Democrats to 35 percent of the district's voters. "There's no point in going to your friends and asking for money unless you think you can win," Case explained to the *Ventura County Star*.

Indeed, of the fifty-three California U.S. House races in 2002, only the Eighteenth District would be competitive, and that had little to do with Michael Berman's map. Over the summer of 2001, Democratic U.S. House member Gary Condit faced controversy about his relationship with his twenty-four-year-old former intern, Chandra Levy, who disappeared and was later found murdered in Rock Creek Park in Washington, DC. Dennis Cardoza, a former Condit aide, would unseat Condit the following year in the Democratic primary and go on to beat the Republican nominee in the general election.

No more than 17 of the 153 U.S. House, State Senate, and State Assembly seats at stake in California in 2002 were considered competitive, compared with 44 competitive seats following the 1991 redistricting. Anne Henderson, legislative director for the League of Women Voters of California, spoke against the new map, claiming it "says that voter participation doesn't matter much." But many politicians portrayed the plan as a model of bipartisan cooperation. "I understand it's not a perfect plan," Democratic Speaker of the Assembly Bob Hertzberg told the *Los Angeles Times*, adding that the plan was "done on a bipartisan basis in the most open way in the history of California."

Even though his own district was safe, Republican Assemblyman Tim Leslie was one of the few legislators openly critical of the plan. Leslie told the *Los Angeles Times*: "We won't have to worry about elections for six, eight, ten years because [the districts] are all pre-set. Everybody wins. . . . What happened to drawing lines for the people of the state rather than ourselves?"

Less than a month after Democratic Governor Gray Davis signed the new redistricting plan, the Mexican American Legal Defense and Educational Fund (MALDEF) filed a voting-rights lawsuit. The group charged that the boundaries for a half-dozen districts were designed to dilute Latino votes and to keep white incumbents in power. Perhaps the most notable challenge involved the district represented by Michael Berman's older brother— Democratic U.S. House member Howard Berman. Howard, by now a twenty-year Anglo veteran of the House, had spearheaded liberal legislation such as farmworker protections. In a 1998 Democratic primary election, the Latino mayor of San Fernando, Raul Godinez, challenged Congressman Berman. Although three out of four Latinos voted for Godinez, Berman won handily by receiving nine out of ten white votes. Michael Berman's new U.S. House map removed Latino voters from his brother's district and put them in an adjacent district represented by another white Democrat, reducing Congressman Berman's voting constituency from 45 percent Latino to 31 percent. Howard Berman defended his district. "For 30 years in public office, I have not merely voted for, but have led the legislative battles to enact issues of importance to the Latino community," he stated. "I guess for MALDEF, it's more about skin color and ethnicity than the philosophy and the quality of representation."

Michael Berman explained to the *Los Angeles Times* that his congressional map protected incumbents of both parties to avoid a bitter partisan split and the possibility of a judicially drawn map. But he also insisted that, overall, his plan "massively protected Latino voting power" statewide.

Indeed, the new map created an additional majority-Hispanic, solidly Democratic district in Los Angeles. Congresswoman Loretta Sanchez—who had insisted that "smart" incumbent Democrats should pay Michael Berman $20,000 for a "district they can win"—helped her sister, Linda, raise money and win the new seat in 2002. And of California's twenty-six Latino state legislators, twenty-three voted for the new maps. But MALDEF President and Chief Counsel Antonia Hernandez told the *Los Angeles Times* that Latino legislators voted for the plans "because their interests [in their own reelections] were taken care of." A federal court dismissed MALDEF's claim in June 2002, in part because it failed to find racially polarized voting in the area's elections outside of Mayor Godinez's challenge to Congressman Berman.

In the November 2002 election, Michael Berman's handiwork paid off. Of the incumbents who ran, 100 percent won reelection. The padding of districts also ensured that most races were not close. The average incumbent won with 69 percent of the vote.

The following year, disgruntled voters recalled Democratic California Governor Gray Davis and replaced him with body-builder and actor Arnold Schwarzenegger, a moderate Republican. But in 2004, all of the incumbent state legislators or U.S. House members who ran retained their seats. Not one of the 100 state legislative seats or 53 U.S. House seats at stake shifted parties.

In 2005, Governor Schwarzenegger supported a redistricting reform plan to shift district-drawing responsibility from state legislators to a panel of retired judges. Voters had rejected a similar reform proposal in 1990, thanks in part to an opposition campaign managed by Michael Berman's consulting firm. A cornerstone of Berman's 1990 effort was a thirty-second television spot that depicted the redistricting proposal as a measure that would empower big oil polluters. "Now that the world is waking up to the environmental threat," the actor in the advertisement announced, "corporate polluters and politicians are spending millions to turn back the clock." San Mateo County Supervisor and former Common Cause activist Tom Huening, a Republican, responded: "It's the most misleading ad I have ever seen in my life." In defense of the commercial, the California director of the Sierra Club asserted that removing redistricting from the hands of politicians would result in fewer environment-friendly legislators.

By 2005, politicians in Sacramento were skeptical about Governor Schwarzenegger's proposal for redistricting reform. "No one has yet approached me and told me that their No. 1 concern is the way legislative boundaries are drawn," said Democratic Assemblyman Tom Umberg, who became chair of the State Assembly redistricting committee in 2004. "They seem to be much more concerned about education, transportation and health care."[2]

In November 2005, California voters rejected the redistricting commission initiative. Many voters associated the redistricting proposal with three other Schwarzenegger-supported initiatives that limited state spending, heightened tenure requirements for school teachers, and curbed union political spending, and saw the package as a Republican power grab. Further, the design of the proposed redistricting commission was flawed, with members consisting of three retired judges (although most California residents are people of color, only about 13 percent of retired California judges are people of color). Voters were also uncomfortable with the fact that the redistricting initiative proposed mid-decade redistricting, which veered from the normal practice of redistricting at the beginning of the decade following the census count. Many civil rights and grass-roots groups opposed the initiative because they believed that a better redistricting commission could be created. In the aftermath of the defeat, groups that opposed the initiative mobilized to craft a ballot initiative with a more diverse and representative commission.

California lawmakers were not the first to draw districts to shape a political outcome. Although it is often regarded as a modern convention, gerrymandering has a 300-year history in the United States. As early as 1705—when members of the Pennsylvania legislature drew district lines to reduce the importance of Philadelphia—politicians manipulated district lines for political gain. The United States Supreme Court recently noted that "Patrick Henry attempted (unsuccessfully) to gerrymander James Madison out of the First Congress." The term *gerrymander* did not arise, however, until 1812, when Massachusetts Governor Elbridge Gerry's party drew a redistricting map that benefited itself and featured one district shaped like a salamander. Political cartoonist Elkanah Tisdale's depiction of the map added some dragonlike fangs, claws, and wings to the odd district, and Tisdale dubbed the creation a "Gerry-mander."

In recent decades, sophisticated computer programs have empowered politicians in California and elsewhere to devise even more creative, precise, and aggressive gerrymanders. Samuel Hirsch is a Washington, DC, lawyer who represents Democrats in districting disputes. According to him, forty-nine congressional districts where both Democratic and Republican candidates had a competitive chance to win were significantly redrawn following the 2000 U.S. Census. Ninety-two percent of incumbents representing these areas obtained safer districts and only 8 percent received more competitive districts. As a result, in the 2004 elections, 98 percent of incumbents running for Congress retained their seats.

Democrats and Republicans do not always collude to protect incumbents from both parties. Sometimes the party in power strengthens its grip by manipulating district lines. For example, with the GOP in control of both the Texas legislature and the governor's mansion, Republican Congressman Tom DeLay orchestrated an unprecedented mid-decade redrawing of Texas districts to pick up additional seats in the U.S. Congress for his party. Republicans reasoned that they were underrepresented by a court-drawn plan adopted after the 2000 Census. In 2002, for example, 53 percent of Texas voters cast their ballots for Republican congressional candidates, but Republicans controlled only 47 percent of the Texas congressional seats. By drawing districts that snaked hundreds of miles across various counties, Republicans inflated their power so that following the 2004 election, they controlled 66 percent of the Texas congressional seats. Among the unseated Democrats was Martin Frost, a longtime critic of DeLay and the only Jewish congressman in the history of the state.

Redistricting is a significant part of the largely invisible matrix of election practices that influences our lives. Politicians, political consultants, lobbyists, and journalists who cover politics pay close attention to the redrawing of district boundaries, because they know that the shapes of districts will determine the balance of power between Democrats and Republicans, as well as which incumbent politicians will cruise to victory without campaigning and which will be vulnerable to challenge. But most voters ignore redistricting, often unaware of its importance in shaping policy and reducing the value of an individual citizen's vote. Politicians who benefit often play down redistricting. In 2001, for example, Republicans controlled all three branches of Michigan's government and drafted legislative maps that expanded their party's power in both chambers. The House of Representatives had just one hearing on the plan that ended at 11 P.M. on July 10, and the House passed the bill with little fanfare at 2:35 A.M. on July 11. Governor John Engler signed the redistricting measure into law two months later—on September 11, just hours after the terrorist attacks in New York and Washington.

Some politicians and scholars argue that incumbent-protection redistricting plans—like in California—produce better representation for voters. An incumbent legislator often has better contacts and more experience and is more likely to hold an important position, such as a committee chairmanship. Competitive elections also drive up campaign costs, making politicians more dependent upon large contributors. Finally, a relatively insulated legislature serves as a moderating check on a president or governor who responds to the whims of the masses.

If incumbents are so golden, however, why should we even hold legislative elections? In China, for example, the Communist Party nominates a candidate for a local position who runs unopposed, and voters cast ballots for the candidate. If most voters approve, the candidate takes office. If voters disapprove, the Communist Party nominates someone else and holds another election. The Chinese system produces long-serving, well-connected politicians who understand the issues, as well as relatively inexpensive elections.

Americans reject the Chinese system, however, because we believe that electoral competition among multiple candidates creates a government that is more responsive to the people. As candidates debate various issues, citizens prioritize our nation's most pressing challenges and formulate their own thoughts about the best solutions. In the words of New York University Professor Ronald Dworkin, individual autonomy involves choice—"a right [of individuals] to make important decisions defining their own lives for themselves." Voters can assess for themselves the benefits of a particular incumbent's experience and contacts. Politicians diminish this choice through their manipulation of electoral rules for partisan gain.[3]

WHEN THE REFEREE PLAYS FAVORITES

Floridians cast six million ballots in the November 2000 presidential election. At the end of the night, Republican George W. Bush led Democrat Al Gore by just 1,784 votes. In accordance with state law, Florida conducted a statewide machine recount, which left Bush ahead by only 300 votes.

At that point, the Gore team focused on four heavily Democratic counties—Broward, Miami-Dade, Palm Beach, and Volusia. An initial manual recount of a few precincts within each of the four counties—in which election workers examined each ballot by hand—showed vote totals different from the machine count. Each of the four counties decided on a manual recount of all ballots.

Florida Secretary of State Katherine Harris—a Republican who also served as cochair of the Bush-Cheney campaign—objected to the countywide manual recounts. She cited with unnerving specificity that Florida law states that counties can do a hand recount of all ballots if the sample manual recount of a few precincts "indicates an error in the vote tabulation. . . ." Harris argued that this phrase allowed a countywide manual recount *only* when the *machinery or software* used in counting the ballots malfunctioned.

Harris, the granddaughter of a Florida citrus and cattle baron, was a trim, forty-three-year-old brunette. Her creamy red lipstick and long black eyelashes attracted attention from the press and late-night comedians. State disclosure records indicated that Harris had a personal net worth of $6.5 million, but her fifty-five-year-old husband, Swedish businessman Sven Anders Axel Ebbeson, was reported to be worth much more. The two married in 1996 while Harris was a state senator; in 1998, she ousted an incumbent secretary of state in the Republican primary and went on to win the general election. During her first two years on the job, Harris spent the bulk of her energy on responsibilities unrelated to election oversight, such as promoting trade between Florida and foreign countries. From the beginning of the primary season, she had been supportive of the Bush nomination, traveling with a group of Florida Republicans to New Hampshire to campaign for him. "I am thrilled and honored to announce my support of George W.

Bush for the presidency," Harris pronounced in a statement featured on the Bush-Cheney Web site.

Democratic Attorney General Bob Butterworth—state chair of the Gore campaign—disagreed with Harris on her assessment of the manual recount. He asserted that "error in the vote tabulation" covered *not only machinery error* but also situations where the machines failed to read ballots that the human eye could read. The case ended up before the Florida Supreme Court, which eventually ruled against Secretary Harris and permitted the countywide recount.

Harris attracted more controversy when she refused to accept vote totals from Democratic counties that failed to complete manual hand counts within a week. Florida law states that counties must submit their election results to the secretary of state seven days after the election, which would have been November 14. Gore's lawyers argued that Harris should extend this deadline because Florida law also provided for countywide manual recounts, which would likely not be completed in Broward, Miami-Dade, Palm Beach, and Volusia one week after the election. Harris, however, announced that she would reject any vote totals submitted after November 14, explaining in a statement:

> The electoral process is a balance between the desire of each voter to have his or her vote recorded and the right of the public to a clear, final result within a reasonable time. It is the duty of the Florida Legislature to strike that balance, and it has done so. The law unambiguously states when the process of counting and recounting the votes cast on Election Day must end. . . .
>
> The Legislature obviously specifically contemplated close elections; the law provides for automatic recounts, protests and manual recounts—and it plainly states when this process must end.

Democrats accused Harris of partisan decisionmaking. Phone records would later reveal that Harris was in contact with the Bush-

Cheney presidential campaign and with Republican Florida Governor Jeb Bush during the contested period following the 2000 election. "Her plan, I'm afraid, has the look of an effort to produce a particular result in the election rather than to ensure that the voice of all the citizens of the state would be heard," said Warren Christopher, Gore spokesperson and former United States secretary of state. "It also looks like a move in the direction of partisan politics and away from the nonpartisan administration of the election laws." Dottie Kormis, a senior citizen who had moved to Palm Beach County from New York, was less diplomatic. "Bush is not trying to steal the election," Ms. Kormis told the *Financial Times*. "Harris is trying to steal it for him."

Others defended Harris. "She's courageous and brave," said sixty-seven-year-old Frank Tomanelli while sporting a pro-Harris T-shirt. "Her decision was independent. She did what she thought the law said, while the other side is just out to destroy anyone who goes against Democrats. To me, she's a hero."

Both Palm Beach and Volusia Counties challenged Harris's refusal to accept vote totals submitted after Tuesday, November 14. On that day, Judge Terry Lewis issued a vague ruling that said Harris "may ignore . . . late filed returns, but may not do so arbitrarily, rather, only by the proper exercise of discretion after consideration of all appropriate facts and circumstances." After the court issued its opinion, Harris rejected the requests by Palm Beach, Broward, and Miami-Dade Counties to submit amended totals at a later date when they completed manual vote counts. On Tuesday, November 21, the Florida Supreme Court reversed Harris's rejection of the manual vote counts, holding that Harris had abused her discretion. The court ordered Harris to accept vote totals until Sunday, November 26.

Palm Beach County failed to finish its manual count by November 26, and Harris denied the county's request for an extension. That evening, Harris arrived in the cabinet room of the

Florida State House, clad in a hunter-red suit jacket, to make a formal announcement to the press and the public. She proclaimed that George W. Bush had won by 537 votes, and that her office "conducted itself with integrity and independence." In conclusion, Harris stated:

> Finally, I wish to point out that our American democracy has triumphed once again. And this is a victory in which we can also take a great deal of pride and comfort. The true winner in the election is the rule of law. Thank you and may God bless America.

Over the next three weeks, the Florida Supreme Court ordered a statewide manual recount, but the U.S. Supreme Court overruled the Florida court and prevented any further tallying of votes. That left no recourse for Gore, and the election was concluded with Bush ahead by 537 votes.

In thirty-three states, the secretary of state or some other elections director is an elected partisan like Katherine Harris. In many other states, the functional head of the state Republican or Democratic Party—the governor—appoints the state elections director and/or a commission to administer elections. And partisanship exists not only at the top. In many states, county election clerks, supervisors, and boards run for their positions in partisan elections or are appointed by partisans.

Partisan election administrators across the nation make countless decisions both before and after elections that can determine election outcomes. In the immediate aftermath of the 2000 election, for example, many Republicans (and a majority of U.S. Supreme Court justices) were concerned that Democratic county election supervisors would twist Florida's "clear intent of the voter" standard in their manual recount of votes to manufacture a Gore victory. Indeed, in a study of the ballots after the election, Democratic counters were 25 percent more likely to deny that a vote was for Bush than Republican counters.

In 2004, Missouri's Republican secretary of state (and candidate for governor), Matt Blunt, insisted on moving an anti–gay-marriage initiative scheduled for the August primary election back to November, when Blunt and President George W. Bush would both appear on the ballot. Pundits speculated that an anti–gay-marriage initiative in November would attract a large number of conservative voters to the polls and boost the ballots cast for gubernatorial candidate Blunt and for President Bush. In a 6–1 vote, the Missouri Supreme Court ruled against Blunt.

While legislators who gerrymander districts generally admit to considering politics, partisans who administer elections often claim neutrality. Katherine Harris's chief of staff, for example, said that accusations of bias were "completely unfounded," and that Harris was simply "maintaining the integrity of the process." But as Terry Madonna, director of the Center for Politics and Public Affairs at Franklin & Marshall College, observed, "Whatever they say about trying to be impartial, [election administrators] are, in effect, partisan. It doesn't mean they're crooked or unfair. But it also doesn't mean that when given a choice they won't render a decision in favor of their party."

There are exceptions. Republican Secretary of State Sam Reed, for example, certified Democrat Christine Gregoire as the winner in Washington state's extremely close gubernatorial race in 2004. Disgruntled Republicans questioned Reed's loyalty and judgment and filed an unsuccessful lawsuit to recall him. "There are some people who have been dismayed that I wasn't a Katherine Harris who took the position, 'I'm a Republican, and by God that comes first,' " the sixty-four-year-old Reed said. "[B]ut I felt that I had to play it straight. I fought the Democrats when I thought they were wrong and I fought the Republicans when I thought they were wrong."

Despite the fact that some partisan election officials make discretionary decisions against their political affiliation, most other democracies in the world recognize the conflict of interest inherent in partisan oversight of elections, and they take concrete steps to address it. More than half of the world's democracies use independent officials or commissions to administer elections, including Australia, Brazil, Canada, India, Iraq, Mexico, Russia, South Africa, and the United Kingdom. Another quarter of the world's democracies allow the government to manage elections but have an oversight body composed primarily of judges, including France, Germany, Spain, Argentina, Japan, New Zealand, and Israel.[4]

OF THE PEOPLE?

> We here highly resolve . . . that government of the people, by the people, for the people, shall not perish from the earth.
>
> —Abraham Lincoln, *Gettysburg Address*, 1863

In the aftermath of the terrorist attacks on the World Trade Center and the Pentagon on September 11, 2001, the United States invested billions of dollars promoting representative democracy in Iraq and Afghanistan. Yet many politicians in the United States enhance their power by undermining the right to vote in America.

Despite their perpetual smiles and perfect sound bites, pragmatic politicians and their agents use rules to shape the electorate and win elections. Some philosophers have even asserted that the people never rule, and that "democracy" is simply a "political formula" that a class of elites uses to justify its rule over a rather poorly informed public. Successful politicians rarely use these words in public to describe American democracy, but few of them are naïve. Most would rather have election rules and practices that benefit themselves and their political party rather than their opponents.

Some might argue that the problem is collusion among the parties that leads to incumbent protection in places such as California. As long as both parties try hard to topple each other—Democrats in Texas, for example, work to scale back Republican congressional seats, and both parties fight each another in election disputes such as Florida 2000—we have no problem. But this approach—which fosters competition at the expense of all other values—gives political parties, officials, candidates, and political operatives the starring roles in democracy and treats voters as mere props to be manipulated. It does not contemplate that voters can make autonomous choices and drive policy.

With regard to redistricting, many nations avoid extreme partisan gerrymandering by employing proportional representation, which does not require single-member districts but instead allows voters to choose their own communities of interest at the ballot box. In the January 2005 elections in Iraq, for example, the major Kurdish parties received 26 percent of the nationwide vote, which entitled them to about the same percentage of the seats in the National Assembly. Ireland and Australia use a different form of proportional representation, in which each voter ranks candidates in order of choice (1, 2, 3, 4, etc.). If a voter's first choice has too little support to win, his vote is transferred to his second-choice candidate. A third form of proportional representation is cumulative voting. Imagine, for example, that a state is entitled to five seats in the U.S. House of Representatives. A voter would be allowed five votes and could cast all five for one congressional candidate or vote for five different candidates—or any combination in between. The five candidates who received the most votes would be elected to Congress. Critics claim that proportional representation is too difficult for voters to understand and that it empowers extremist minority groups while depriving the majority of the right to rule. While these concerns are overstated and overlook the fact that certain states and localities in the United States have used proportional representation for years, widespread use of proportional representation may be politically infeasible in the United States at this juncture.[5]

Empowering voters is difficult, and any such attempt is fraught with both attacks by incumbent politicians and the existence of political operatives who resist surrendering their control over the matrix. Below, I've sketched out a few options designed to restore control to voters. None is perfect, but all are better than the status quo.

1. A New Mapmaker

Independent commissions, rather than politicians, should take responsibility for drawing the boundaries of districts. Almost all democracies in the world that use single-member districts to elect legislators assign responsibility for drawing districts to independent commissions, including Australia, Canada, Germany, New Zealand, and the United Kingdom. By removing this responsibility from elected politicians, appointed commissions diminish the likelihood that the objectives of political elites—such as party dominance and incumbent protection—will be the primary drivers of district boundaries.

Some American scholars and partisans question the value of assigning election oversight to independent nonpartisan officials. University of Pennsylvania law professor Nathaniel Persily, for example, observes that "appointed officials will be beholden to those appointing them or at least selected because their intentions are well known." Republican U.S. House member John T. Doolittle of California told the *New York Times*: "Redistricting is inherently political. . . . All you're going to do [through a commission] is submerge the politics."

Granted, independent election officials will be only as good as the process of selecting them. In America, a few states use a commission to draw districts, including Arizona, Hawaii, Idaho, Iowa, Montana, New Jersey, and Washington. But evidence suggests that many of these commissions are not truly independent, and that politicians can easily stack the commission with party insiders like political consultant Michael Berman to do their bidding. For example, in New Jersey, four partisan leaders within the state legislature and the chairs of the state Democratic and Republican Parties each appoint two members.

A different process would increase independence. Rather than allowing partisan politicians to have sole appointment power, any citizen should be able to apply. An applicant might be *ineligible* to serve on a commission if, over the previous five years, he or she:

a) had served as an employee or independent contractor of an elected official, candidate, or political party;

b) had held a leadership position in a political party;

c) had run as a candidate or served in elective office;

d) had worked as a registered lobbyist; or

e) had given a total of more than $5,000 to local, state, and federal candidates.

Close relatives of anyone meeting the above criteria should also be disqualified from commission service. A panel of judges could screen applicants to ensure each could be fair (just as judges scrutinize jurors to ensure fairness). Applicants might be divided into three categories—Republicans, Democrats, and Independents. At that point, there would be a random selection (a lottery) from each pool of applicants to create a commission of three Democrats, four Independents, and three Republicans. Any redistricting plan would require a supermajority vote of eight of the ten commission members. Anyone serving on the commission would be barred for five years from running for office or serving as a registered lobbyist.

This selection process is not the only one that could work, but it does show that measures exist to enhance the independence of a commission. Even a commission with strong procedural safeguards may not be completely free of prejudices—just as juries and judges are never completely immune. The test of independent redistricting, however, is not whether it completely eliminates bias but rather whether it reduces the personal and professional stake that decisionmakers have in the political outcome.[6]

2. A Better Umpire

All states should appoint an independent chief elections officer to administer elections. Professor Richard Hasen at Loyola Law School, a coauthor of one of the leading election-law textbooks, has perhaps the best proposal. A secretary of state or other chief elections officer who runs in even a nonpartisan election is likely to rely on the party machinery to get elected, and a chief elections officer appointed by a partisan governor is likely to be tainted. In light of these problems, Hasen proposes that the chief elections officer be nominated by the governor and approved by a supermajority— perhaps 75 percent—of the legislature. Giving the minority party such veto power would ensure a "consensus candidate who is seen as above politics." The elections officer should be immunized from political pressure by giving him or her a single long term without the possibility of reappointment and a budget guaranteed by the state constitution. To ensure that the governor and the legislature agree on a manager rather than a political operative, an additional safeguard would require that nominees for chief elections officer meet the prerequisites articulated above for service on an independent redistricting commission (i. e., no candidates, elected officials, lobbyists, party officials, large campaign contributors, or independent contractors or employees of politicians—or their close relatives—need apply). The officer should also be barred from significant political activity during his or her term—such as serving as chair of a presidential campaign. Professor Hasen cites Canada and Australia as nations in which independent election administrators take pride in their neutrality and have significant credibility among the citizenry.

Recognizing that bias can be reduced, the most compelling argument against an appointed chief elections official or an independent redistricting commission seems to be that elected partisans face voters. The National Association of Secretaries of State defended its members' capacity to administer elections fairly by observing that "our constituents have the opportunity to vote us out of office if they are unhappy with what we are doing." Why should voters trust unelected independent bureaucrats over a state legislature and secretary of state who must face voters and account for their actions? Democracy is an empty promise, the argument goes, if voters cannot elect those who will make decisions about the rules and structure of democracy. Appointed, independent oversight of democracy can seem antidemocratic and paternalistic.

Taken to its logical conclusion, however, this argument would do away with a host of devices that minimize conflicts of interest, such as campaign contribution limits and restrictions on the personal gifts that lawmakers and elected judges can receive, because citizens could simply vote against a corrupt official. Rather than making every election a referendum on the fairness of politicians, however, we should shift election oversight responsibilities to independent officials and free the politicians to focus on such partisan issues as establishing tax policy, providing for health care, and chairing presidential campaigns.

And we should not assume that an independent approach will always be less democratic. Incumbent legislators who draw their own entrenching districts are not particularly accountable to voters. A chief elections officer who is approved by 75 percent of the state legislature is more accountable to a broad array of a state's population than a secretary of state appointed by a partisan governor without such approval. Finally, to the extent that voters approve ballot questions that call for independent election oversight, we should recognize that such measures can advance rather than thwart the will of the people.[7]

3. Empowering Citizens

In addition to an independent redistricting commission and a chief elections officer, states should also regularly appoint citizen assemblies to make recommendations about democratic reforms.

Independent elections officials address conflict-of-interest problems, but they do little to integrate citizens into the process. While this shortcoming is largely practical (it is difficult to get fifteen million Californians into one room to determine where to draw district boundaries and which punch card ballots to count), states should establish regular citizen assemblies to allow for more involvement by average people.

A citizen assembly would consist of a randomly selected group of average voters (much like a jury, but larger). The assembly would investigate election problems and hear testimony from citizens, political scientists, local and state politicians, and election administrators from other states and nations. The assembly would then draft election reforms that would go on the ballot for voters to approve or reject in states with a ballot-initiative process.

In states without a ballot-initiative process, the citizen assembly would submit its reform proposals directly to the state legislature, and politicians would have to vote the proposals up or down. The power of the citizen assembly would come largely from its credibility with the public—much like that of the 9/11 Commission that proposed intelligence and national-security reforms in the aftermath of the 2001 terrorist attacks. If the assembly conducted an open and fair process, proposed reasonable reforms, and enjoyed extensive credibility with voters, politicians might be hesitant to vote against the reforms, and some might even champion them. The Canadian province of British Columbia has spearheaded the concept of citizen assemblies, and Australia and the United Kingdom both have influential bodies that make recommendations about election reforms.[8]

Enhancing the independence of election officials and facilitating more citizen-driven election reforms is only part of the puzzle. We still need to address inequalities in funding, voting machines, and other aspects of democracy that arise from county to county across the United States.

CHAPTER TWO

PATCHWORK DEMOCRACY

Tanya Thivener, a thirty-eight-year-old mortgage broker in Columbus, Ohio, knew the wait would be long when she arrived at her neighborhood poll on November 2, 2004. The line snaked out the door. Ohio was a swing state, and the electoral meltdown in Florida four years earlier showed that every vote mattered. Tanya waited an hour in the rain. And then she waited some more.

But many of Tanya's neighbors lacked either flexibility with their bosses at work or patience. "A lot of people left in the four hours I waited," Tanya told the *Washington Post*. "A lot of them were young black men who were saying over and over: 'We knew this would happen.' "

After Tanya voted, she drove to her mother's house in Harrisburg, a suburb of Columbus. Her mother reported that voting had taken only fifteen minutes at her neighborhood poll. "[Franklin] County officials knew they had this huge increase in registrations, and yet there weren't enough machines in the city," Tanya said. "You really hope this wasn't intentional."

But some suburban polls in Franklin County were jammed as well. In Grove City, eighty-year-old Dorothy Eloise Turner arrived at and left her Finland Elementary School polling place twice, discouraged by the long lines. On her third visit, she concluded that the lines weren't getting any shorter and decided to stay. For most of the next two and a half hours, Mrs. Turner stood in line in the rain. Chairs were not offered to elderly voters—everyone waited on their feet—and the standing started to strain her back. As nightfall approached, she asked a few other voters if she could jump ahead of them because she was uncomfortable driving after dark, and they agreed. "I wanted to wait with them because I don't know if I will be here for the next presidential election," Mrs. Turner told the *Columbus Dispatch*. "In my whole lifetime, I never saw anything like I did [Tuesday]."

At some precincts, poll workers tried to speed up lines by enforcing an obscure state law that limited voters to five minutes in the polling booth. But lengthy ballots made compliance difficult. In Columbus, for example, more than forty candidates and issues crammed the ballot.

Some attributed the long lines to an increase in newly registered voters with little experience casting ballots. Others, like Summit County Elections Director Bryan Williams, looked to poll workers. "The lines are determined by the quality of your booth workers," Williams said. And yet others blamed federal reforms enacted after the 2000 presidential election to ensure that poll workers would not mistakenly turn away any voter. The Help America Vote Act requires that states provide provisional ballots to voters who do not appear on the voter rolls; ballots of those voters later deemed eligible are counted. "The biggest source of congestion was the provisional ballot," Aaron Epstein, a Franklin County Democratic Party poll observer, told the *Columbus Dispatch*. "It took at least twice as long to vote on a provisional ballot."

But most agreed that large voter turnout and too few voting machines played the most significant roles in lengthening the lines. Both parties knew that Ohio could go to either Republican George W. Bush or Democrat John Kerry, so the parties worked hard to register supporters and get them to the polls. In Franklin County alone, 102,000 new voters had been added to the registration rolls.

And some counties provided too few voting machines. Summit County—home to the city of Akron—sits two hours north of Franklin County up Interstate 71. Its voting wards averaged 86 voters per machine, compared with Franklin County's 170 voters per machine. The longest lines in Summit County were ninety minutes, while Franklin County had five-hour lines.

The disparities between Summit and Franklin stemmed from different decisions by county election officials. Each Ohio county has a four-person elections board (two Republicans and two Democrats) that determines the number and distribution of voting machines. In Summit County, the Board of Elections aspired to have at least one voting machine for every 100 registered voters. To meet their goal, Summit County rented 600 additional machines and took another 500 out of storage.

In contrast, the members of the Franklin County Board of Elections determined that they needed 5,000 machines to accommodate voters, yet they decided to ride out Election Day with just 2,866 machines. "Does it make any sense to purchase more machines just for one election?" Democrat Michael R. Hackett, the deputy director of the Franklin County Board of Elections, asked a *Washington Post* reporter. "I'll give you the answer: no."

Instead of purchasing or renting additional machines, the Franklin County board decided to rearrange machines. It moved machines from urban areas in Columbus to its suburbs. As a result, about half of Franklin County's 146 wards had fewer voting machines than in 2000. The elections board's director, Republican Matthew Damschroder, explained that the county moved the machines because of suburban population growth. "We have the same number of machines, but they had to be spread over more precincts," Damschroder said. The shuffling of machines was not based on the number of registered voters—which had increased in many urban areas—but instead on previous turnout in each precinct.

As a result, conservative suburban precincts in Franklin County tended to have *more* machines per *registered voter* than the more liberal urban areas. But in the suburbs, more voters cast a ballot on each machine than in urban areas. It is unclear whether the lower turnout per machine in urban areas was caused in part by inner-city voters who were less able or willing to stand in four-hour lines. Many frustrated people "walked away without voting," Scott Britton, executive director of the nonpartisan League of Women Voters of Ohio, told the *Columbus Dispatch*. "I don't think we'll ever know how many there were."

The fact that voters in Franklin County faced much longer lines than voters in Summit County illustrates a larger problem. An American's right to vote and have the ballot counted depends on where he or she lives. Voters in almost every other democracy in the world enjoy a more equal opportunity to cast a ballot. Why? Because the United States is one of the few nations where local officials—who often also represent a political party—enjoy extensive control over elections for federal, state, and local officeholders. National officials, for example, administer all elections in France, Italy, Portugal, South Africa, and South Korea. Even in nations such as Canada and Australia, which have some local administration, federal officials almost always administer elections for national offices and either oversee or work closely with provincial or local officials who administer elections for provincial and local positions.

In the United States, however, each state adopts its own requirements for voting and conducting elections. States further decentralize the process and give election administration responsibility to county, city, and township governments, which in turn adopt their own unique practices. While responsibilities vary, secretaries of state often administer state election laws. In almost all states, town or county clerks and auditors maintain official voter-registration lists and oversee absentee voting. In several states, town or county "election boards" or "boards of canvassers" focus on Election Day activities by maintaining and distributing voting machines, selecting and staffing polling locations, and counting ballots. Thus, the matrix comprises hundreds of election rules and practices that vary from state to state, and often from county to county. Americans do not have a single uniform set of rules for voting, or even 50 separate state election systems—effectively, there are 4,600 different election systems. While almost all other nations have given their citizens a clearly established constitutional right to vote, U.S. constitutional provisions prohibit only discrimination in voting based on race, gender, and similar factors. Thus, in America, your "right" to vote depends largely on the inclinations of your state and local politicians and bureaucrats.[1]

For example, on Election Day 2004, Brandi Stenson went with her mother and brother to their local polling place at St. Elizabeth Seton School in Toledo, Ohio. The Stensons joined one of three lines. When they finally reached the front, the poll worker had bad news. "They looked in the book, and none of our names was there," Brandi told the *Toledo Blade*. The Stensons knew they were registered, and Brandi and her mother started asking questions. But other voters were waiting, so the poll worker gave them provisional ballots. All three voted provisionally. When they returned home, Brandi's sister Brittany said that she had no problems when she voted earlier in the day, and that she had seen the names of the rest of the family in the polling book. "We were in the right building. We were in the wrong lines," Brandi said.

Because the Stensons stood in the Precinct 4N line rather than their assigned precinct's line (which was in the same room), not only were their names missing from the voting rolls but elections officials refused to count their provisional ballots. The Stensons were not alone. Of the sixty-seven provisional ballots cast in

Precinct 4N, fifty were thrown out because voters were in the right room but the wrong precinct line.

"I just feel like they didn't know what they were doing," Brandi said of the poll workers, who never looked up the Stensons' address or offered to direct them to the right precinct line. "They wanted us to hurry up, because I was asking questions, my mom was asking questions. . . . They were trying to rush us out."

Across the United States, a voter's ability to cast a provisional ballot—described by many as the ultimate safety net—varies. Brandi's ballot would have counted had she lived across the state line in Pennsylvania or in another of the two dozen states without Ohio's restrictive rule that excludes provisional votes cast in the wrong precinct. And within a single state like Ohio, nebulous standards for determining voter eligibility allow election officials in one county to reject a provisional ballot that could be counted in another county. Voter-registration deadlines also vary from state to state. Idaho and Wisconsin offer Election Day voter registration at the polls. But you must register ten days before an election in Alabama and Iowa, twenty days before in Massachusetts and Utah, and thirty days in Alaska and Mississippi.

Four years after Florida's hanging-chad fiasco, only 13.1 percent of American voters used punch-card machines, but more than 70 percent of Ohio voters used such machines. Punch-card ballots have a much higher rate of spoilage—where either no presidential candidate is selected or more than one presidential candidate is punched—than other ballots. Several studies established that punch-card spoilage rates are more than three times higher in precincts with more lower-income individuals and more people of color than in areas with higher incomes and few people of color. Ohio punch-card machines produced more than 76,000 spoiled ballots in November 2004 (a smaller number than President Bush's 118,600-vote margin of victory over Senator Kerry).

And you'll need to do some legal research if you're one of the thirteen million Americans who have been convicted of a felony. Maine allows prisoners to vote. Illinois limits voting to people outside of prison. Former offenders in Louisiana can vote only if they have fully completed their sentence, including probation and parole. And Florida puts a lifetime ban on voting by people who have committed a felony, including those who have served their time. (I'll discuss the felon issue in more detail later in this chapter.)[2]

THE CONSTITUTION AND THE MATRIX

While the Tenth Amendment of the U.S. Constitution reserves to the states all powers not specifically delegated to the federal government, a host of constitutional provisions assign the federal government critical responsibility for protecting democracy. The Elections Clause authorizes states to establish the time, place, and manner of federal elections, but it also gives the federal government the authority to "make or alter such Regulations." The Spending Clause empowers Congress to spend for the "general welfare," and the federal government has wide latitude to condition receipt of funds on a state's compliance with basic democratic standards. The Constitution mandates that "the United States shall guarantee to every State in this Union a Republican Form of Government," which presumably means that Congress can void state and local practices that undermine representative democracy.

The Fourteenth Amendment authorizes the federal government to ensure that states afford people "equal protection of the laws," and the Fifteenth, Nineteenth, and Twenty-fourth Amendments empower Congress to prevent racial, gender, and wealth discrimination at the polls.

The federal government has weighed in, using its authority to enact laws that rein in state and local election officials to create a more equal and accessible playing field for voters:

1965—*The Voting Rights Act*: Curbs racial exclusion at the polls by prohibiting discriminatory voting practices; explicitly establishes federal involvement in voter registration and other practices previously governed exclusively by states and localities.

1984—*The Voting Accessibility for the Elderly and Handicapped Act*: Requires that states provide accessible polling places to Americans with disabilities for federal elections.

1986—*The Uniformed and Overseas Citizens Absentee Voting Act*: Ensures that U.S. military and other citizens living abroad can vote in federal elections.

1993—*The National Voter Registration Act ("Motor Voter Act")*: Requires that states make voter registration available at the Department of Motor Vehicles and other state offices, and prevents state and local bureaucrats from indiscriminately purging voters from registration lists.

2002—*The Help America Vote Act ("HAVA")*: Requires that states create statewide voter-registration lists and provide provisional ballots at the polls, and creates the Election Assistance Commission to distribute money to states and advise states on election practices.

Not surprisingly, many state and local election administrators are skeptical of federal laws and prefer the freedom to run elections with minimal federal involvement. I was a member of the Carter-Baker Commission on Federal Election Reform, an independent commission cochaired by former President Jimmy Carter and former U.S. Secretary of State James Baker. Kansas Secretary of State Ron Thornburgh appeared before our commission and testified:

> To be a chief state election official today is to walk a tightrope—carefully balancing the needs of your state with the demands of the federal government. . . . [D]espite states' significant election reform progress, there is a movement by some to federalize elections. Let me just say very clearly: the states' biggest fear is a continued expansion of the federal role in elections through regulatory oversight and micromanagement. . . .

Despite Federal election reforms and resistance by some state and local officials, the division of power between the federal government and the states is not clearly established. In 1970, eighteen-year-olds could be drafted to go to Vietnam but could not vote in many states. Congress passed a federal law lowering the voting age to eighteen in federal, state, and local elections, which conflicted with state laws in Arizona, Idaho, Oregon, and Texas requiring that voters be at least twenty-one-years-old. All four states went to the U.S. Supreme Court to challenge the power of Congress to enact the law. The states won over four of the nine Supreme Court justices, who reasoned that states and localities should control voting qualifications in all elections. Another four justices disagreed, concluding that Congress had the power under the Fourteenth Amendment's Equal Protection Clause to extend voting rights to eighteen-year-olds for all elections. Justice Hugo Black, who was the final and deciding vote, split the baby and ruled that the Elections Clause of the Constitution allowed Congress to mandate eighteen-year-old voting for federal offices such as U.S. Senate or president but not for state and local offices. In the same case, all nine justices agreed that Congress could pass laws to prevent racial discrimination in federal, state, and local elections. Six months after the Supreme Court issued its opinion, the Twenty-sixth Amendment to the U.S. Constitution was ratified, lowering the voting age in all federal, state, and local elections to eighteen. But the question of the proper role of federal and state governments in election oversight remained.[3]

In light of the contested division of power between Congress and the states, a frank discussion about the costs and benefits of localism in voting allows us to move past sound bites toward real solutions.

LOCAL TAILORING AND INEQUALITY

Imagine that most Californians support "early convenience voting"—a program that allows busy people to cast ballots at a few central locations during the twenty-nine-day "window" preceding Election Day. Most residents of Pennsylvania, however, object to early voting because they believe that all voters should cast a ballot on a single day when political debate peaks. Pennsylvanians also suspect that early voting drags out voter mobilization and drives up candidates' campaign costs. A single federal rule that either adopted or prohibited early voting would upset either a majority of Californians or a majority of Pennsylvanians—and a compromise offering early voting for fifteen days might disappoint both. Allowing each state to adopt a different rule, the argument goes, keeps the maximum number of Californians and Pennsylvanians happy.

States and local officials can tailor registration requirements, polling places, and voting equipment to satisfy local needs and desires. Such tailoring would be impossible if America used rigid, one-size-fits-all national election rules. In a letter to the United States Congress, the National Association of Secretaries of State explained:

> State governments enjoy a close connection to the people. . . . [T]hat connection means that state governments are best prepared to decide what is right for their residents. What works in New York City, for example, may not be the right solution for a small town in rural Idaho.

Further, tailoring election laws to fit particular localities avoids giving preference to a single vision of democracy over all others. Rather than rejecting either California's twenty-nine-day voter-convenience approach or Pennsylvania's single-day collective-deliberation approach, state and local control of elections allows conflicting democratic visions to coexist.

The problem with such tailoring, however, is that different ballot designs, counting technologies, recount standards, and other local election practices undermine equality if they make voting more difficult for some or make their votes less likely to be counted. As the gap in wait times between Franklin and Summit Counties shows, the ease of voting can vary greatly within a state. Such inconsistencies can undermine access to the polls and the determination of which candidate actually received the most votes, especially in close elections.

While many states fear federal intrusion, electoral uniformity advances constitutional principles. In 1964, for example, the U.S. Supreme Court announced a one-person, one-vote rule that restricted state autonomy by requiring that all of a legislative body's districts within a state contain the same number of voters. Almost four decades later, in the case of *Bush v. Gore*, the U.S. Supreme Court held that the nebulous "clear intent of the voter" standard used by county officials to manually recount ballots violated the Fourteenth Amendment; the Court stopped the recount with George W. Bush ahead by 537 votes. Specifically, the Supreme Court reasoned:

Having once granted the right to vote on equal terms, the State may not, by later arbitrary and disparate treatment, value one person's vote over that of another. . . . [E]ach of the counties used varying standards to determine what was a legal vote. Broward County used a more forgiving standard than Palm Beach County, and uncovered almost three times as many new votes, a result markedly disproportionate to the difference in population between the counties.

Perhaps realizing that manual-recount standards were the tip of the iceberg, and wary of the practical implications of the logic, the justices in *Bush v. Gore* tried to limit their ruling, writing:

> Our consideration is limited to the present circumstances, for the problem of equal protection in election processes generally presents many complexities. . . . The question before the Court is not whether local entities, in the exercise of their expertise, may develop different systems for implementing elections.

Despite this qualification, the *Bush v. Gore* court identified a problem that extends past manual recounts and includes hundreds of election processes that vary from locality to locality. Like a court ordering a recount, state officials enjoy the power to ensure uniformity, equal treatment, and fundamental fairness in the distribution and type of voting machines, ballot design, and other election practices. The U.S. Supreme Court, however, has not yet mandated such equal treatment by states. Regardless of whether local officials are trying to game the election outcome or simply lack financial resources, their different standards and practices inevitably result in hurdles that apply to some voters but not to others. Harvard Professor of Government Jennifer Hochschild concludes that variations in election practices represent "a surprisingly simple and effective way of ensuring that some voters remain political losers." Such variations, she claims, "almost always [act] to the detriment of those with the least education and resources and the most need of gaining political influence." In short, any benefits from the local tailoring of election laws must be balanced against concerns such as threats to equality and widespread voter participation.[4]

LAB RATS

In 1890, Wyoming was the only state that allowed women to vote when it joined the Union that year. By 1920, the successful experiment in Wyoming and several other localities around the nation resulted in the ratification of the Nineteenth Amendment, which guaranteed women the right to vote. Today, innovation by states and localities has also been expanding the franchise. Idaho and Wisconsin, for example, offer Election Day voter registration, and North Dakota has no registration at all. Six towns in Maryland allow noncitizens to vote in elections. While most Illinois counties refused to count a provisional ballot cast outside of a voter's home precinct in a recent election, Cook County (Chicago) officials counted such ballots. Oregon operates its entire election system through mail-in ballots, making voting more convenient and increasing participation.

Rather than risking immediate rejection by a nationwide audience, state and local control of elections gives reformers the opportunity to attain tangible successes on a smaller stage and hone their proposals. Local control also allows a county to test new voting equipment and techniques without jeopardizing elections across the state or nation. In theory, such autonomy also allows states and localities to compete with one another to provide the best election processes.

But experimenting on voters also carries costs. In 2000, Palm Beach County Supervisor of Elections Theresa LePore tried to design a ballot with large type so that it could be read by her county's large senior population. LePore, however, tested her "butterfly ballot" in a real election rather than on sample voters. The confusing ballot caused thousands in Palm Beach County to mistakenly vote for Pat Buchanan, and it cost Al Gore an estimated 6,607 Florida votes and the presidency.

Local innovation without oversight fails to acknowledge that some experiments are unwise or inappropriate. Few voters want to be lab rats. Extensive state and local discretion with minimal oversight mistakenly assumes that Theresa LePore should be the final arbiter of citizens' voting rights.

While a few states like Hawaii and Oregon assume the bulk of election costs, most of America's elections are financed by counties, cities, and towns. Indeed, prior to the Help America Vote Act's allotment of money for voting machine upgrades in 2002, the federal government had never provided funding to help localities administer elections.

A lack of money has a direct impact on voters. A Government Accounting Office study of obstacles faced by voters with disabilities claimed: "[M]ost state election officials told us that limited funding is one of the main barriers to improving voting accessibility, especially with regard to providing more accessible voting equipment." According to former Washington Secretary of State Ralph Munro, the National Association of Secretaries of State failed to adopt a proposal for weekend voting—which would help workers who have inflexible hours or two jobs—in large part because of the cost of paying building custodians to come in on weekends and open polling sites at schools.

Cash-strapped cities and localities do not always attempt to offer the most innovative, accessible, or accurate elections. Instead, they often aspire to provide the cheapest elections, though without attracting the notoriety of Florida's bungling in 2000. Inexpensive elections allow cities and counties to invest greater sums in more visible and quantifiable expenditures that sustain housing values, such as good schools and low crime rates. Localities rarely compete for the best voting system. Rather, the race to the top among localities for better schools and crime prevention is often subsidized by a race to the bottom in administering democracy.

While voters rarely organize to pressure local politicians to spend more on election administration, we cannot allow complacency to promote a cut-rate electoral system. Democracy is not an individual commodity to be bought and sold like a dream house in a safe suburb with good schools. We all lose when individual voters in some areas face long lines and are discouraged from the polls. The legitimacy of government is compromised, and we all become party to the lack of basic human dignity afforded to those whose time and choices are disrespected.[5]

DISTRUST

Currently, local authorities within 4,600 different election districts control American democracy. If we were to centralize authority in a single elections czar who oversaw America's 22,000 election officials, 700,000 voting machines, and 1.4 million poll workers, the czar might skew election practices to favor one political ideology, party, or candidate. Zimbabwe administers its elections on a national level, for example, and several international observers have charged that President Robert Mugabe's incumbent administration—with the help of its national electoral board—rigged election results in the March 2005 elections.

While Zimbabwe is an extreme example, and most centrally administered election systems are credible, a healthy distrust of centralized government justifies distributing some responsibility for elections among states and localities. Just as Congress, the president, and the judiciary check one another, state authority over elections checks federal power, and local administration prevents abuse at the state level. Local control also protects against the tyranny of a majority of Americans from outside the area. As Alexis de Tocqueville wrote in *Democracy in America*, "Municipal bodies and county administrations are like so many hidden reefs retarding or dividing the flood of the popular will."

Further, Americans who register others to vote, work at community polling places, or see their neighbors performing these and other tasks gain a deeper sense of self-government. By providing hands-on democracy training, local control facilitates engagement among citizens. Complete federalization of elections, cutting out local input, would only make citizens even more detached from government, more self-absorbed, and less interested in the common good.

But states'-rights advocates fail to explain why state and local politicians are more trustworthy or competent than federal officials. After the Civil War, Southern whites used local election practices such as literacy tests and poll taxes to exclude African-American voters for almost a century. In Florida during the 2000 election, Republicans were suspicious of the manual recount of punch-card ballots by local Democratic election supervisors, while Democrats across the nation were concerned that a Florida partisan—Republican Secretary of State Katherine Harris—would determine the future of 300 million Americans.

Informality and intimacy on the local level can also facilitate "old boy" networks that monopolize decisionmaking through backroom deals and exclude meaningful participation by citizens. News reporters, government officials, and good-government groups from across the country are likely to watch for and criticize a federal bureaucrat's self-serving manipulation of election law. The "hidden reefs" of 4,600 different election districts, however, can obscure the individual bad acts of local political predators, making abuses difficult to anticipate, detect, and remedy.

While state and local officials may be "close" to the people, they also may be more vested in local politics and tempted to manipulate election rules in a way that disenfranchises voters. Indeed, unchecked state and local authority is more dangerous in the polling booth—where incumbent politicians have incentives to rig the rules to maintain power—than in other areas, such as setting

speed limits on local roads. State rules that prevent former offenders who have completed their sentences from voting illustrate that
some state and local politicians have ulterior motives.

In 1995, Debbie Hardy was a drug addict who had served six
months in jail on a felony charge. She had nine children out of wed-
lock and lost custody of all of them. But then she turned her life
around. She kicked her drug habit and helped her older sister to do
the same. By 2004, she was raising two of her oldest children—with
one bound for the U.S. Navy and the other for college. She also had
a good job as the manager of a Burger King restaurant. Hardy lives in
Florida, however, a state that imposes a lifetime ban on voting by former offenders who have completed their sentences. So Hardy's past
continues to haunt her. "I am trying to do the right thing, but I have
had this felony hanging over my head for twelve years," said Hardy.

An estimated 1.6 million people in the United States have completed their sentences but cannot vote. Despite the fact that 80 percent of Americans favor restoring voting rights to these citizens, the
disenfranchisement persists because some politicians oppose extend-
ing the right to vote to people like Debbie Hardy. "As frank as I can
be," said Alabama Republican Party Chairman Marty Connors in
2003, "we're opposed to [restoring voting rights after completion of
sentence] because felons don't tend to vote Republican." Studies
suggest that just under 70 percent of former felons would vote
Democratic. While restrictive rules in states like Alabama prevent
voting for life by most former felons who have served their time,
Florida, Kentucky, and Virginia permanently prohibit voting by *all*
citizens who have committed a felony. The ban prevents voting by
more than one of every eight African-American adults in these states.

Politicians use "states'-rights" rhetoric to justify these citizens'
continued disenfranchisement. In 2002, Republican U.S. Senator
Mitch McConnell of Kentucky opposed federal legislation extend-
ing the right to vote in federal elections to all former felons who
had completed their sentences. "States have a significant interest in

reserving the vote for those who have abided by the social contract," Senator McConnell explained. "Those who break our laws should not dilute the vote of law-abiding citizens."

But McConnell did not mention that the voting restriction strengthens his political grip in Kentucky. McConnell would have likely lost a tightly contested 1984 U.S. Senate race if it weren't for Kentucky's ban on voting by former felons. Similarly, the restriction allowed the junior senator from Kentucky, Republican Jim Bunning, to eke out a narrow victory in a 1998 Senate contest (Bunning won by only 6,766 votes; Kentucky banned 94,584 former offenders from voting). The outcomes of two other U.S. Senate races since 1978 in Virginia and Florida also would have been different had former felons been allowed to vote. And Al Gore would have won Florida (and thus the presidency) by about 31,000 votes in 2000.

State officials' commitment to denying voting rights to citizens who have completed their sentences also puts the United States out of step with international democratic norms. Many democracies allow inmates to cast ballots while incarcerated, including Australia, Canada, Denmark, France, Germany, Ireland, Israel, Japan, Peru, Poland, South Africa, Spain, and Sweden. Others restore voting rights to prisoners once they complete their sentences, such as in Argentina, Brazil, Egypt, India, Portugal, Russia, and the United Kingdom. According to research sponsored by the International Foundation for Election Systems, Florida, Kentucky, and Virginia are alone with Armenia in being the only democratic governments in the world that permanently revoke voting rights from citizens who have committed any felony, even after they have completed their sentences. As a result of these three Southern states, U.S. citizens account for only 4.6 percent of the world's population but make up almost half of the people on the planet who cannot vote due to a criminal offense.[6]

In short, state and local officials sometimes disenfranchise citizens to inflate their own power.

BALANCING THE SCALES

Both "federal reform" and "states' rights" have become slogans that tug in opposite directions, but neither—by itself—provides much practical insight into how we should craft a democracy that best protects voters.

And the U.S. Supreme Court's approach to the problem provides few clear answers. As mentioned earlier, the justices have been divided on the proper role of federal oversight of elections, and they intervened in state regulatory minutiae to invalidate the manual-recount procedure in *Bush v. Gore*. The Court has also demanded that the federal government's actions be tailored—or "congruent and proportional"—to prevent inequality without unnecessarily infringing on state and local autonomy. This nebulous and generic standard provides little guidance to judges, election-law reformers, and states. An inner-city civil-rights activist, for example, might think that subtle racism at the polls justifies a federal Voting Rights Act. A corporate executive who lives in a ritzy suburb, on the other hand, might look at race as a problem of the past and reject federal intervention.

Recognizing that elections benefit from different traits that federal, state, and local actors are uniquely positioned to provide, we need to figure out what combination of national, state, and local systems best protects our voting rights. How do we obtain the benefits of state and local administration while minimizing the costs?

Perhaps the best approach toward this goal would allow states and localities to run elections but encourage federal involvement that promotes equality and access and prevents political manipulation by state and local politicians. This would give state and local officials the opportunity to address problems unique to a particular community, but it would also hold them accountable when they inadvertently or intentionally disenfranchise voters.

According to Yale Law Professor Akhil Amar, not only did the founders contemplate the states checking the national government, they also envisioned that the national government would protect citizens by checking the states. James Madison wrote in the *Federalist Papers*, Amar explains, that "the rights of the people" are best protected in a system in which federal and state governments "control each other."

A couple of examples illustrate appropriate federal oversight of federal, state, and local elections. The Voting Rights Act enables the federal government to review proposed changes to state and local election practices to ensure that they are not discriminatory. This review is an appropriate exercise of federal power because it serves as a check on potential abuses by local incumbent politicians and ensures access by voters. Similarly, federal provisions that require localities with large limited-English populations to provide bilingual ballots should be deemed appropriate, even for groups without an extensively documented history of discrimination in this country, such as Russian Americans. By ensuring access, bilingual ballots allow citizens to serve as an effective check on politicians. Equality and access concerns would also justify federal laws that remove barriers to voting encountered by people with disabilities (such as the Americans with Disabilities Act). A congressional decision to extend voting rights to former offenders who have completed their sentences in federal, state, and local elections should be respected.

In contrast, a federal proposal to place all responsibility for administering elections in the hands of a single federal bureaucrat— completely displacing state and local governments from these functions—would exceed federal authority. Such a proposal would go beyond being a "check" on local governments and would enhance the possibility of abuse by the federal government. Note that federal "abuse" does not arise every time that state and local politicians disagree with federal actions. The checking function is intended to protect voters from manipulation by federal officials— not to protect an imagined entitlement to make decisions by turf-conscious state and local politicians.

Granted, there will be tough cases in which we debate whether particular federal proposals go too far. Nevertheless, by acknowledging a role for all levels of government and focusing on each level's strengths and weaknesses, we can have a real discussion rather than an exchange of empty sound bites.

One difficult question is whether federal reforms should promote greater centralized control by state authorities. On one hand, delegating supervisory responsibility to the state enhances accountability. Without such a clear delegation, states can blame problems on localities, and localities can claim they are simply volunteer workers who lack the resources to run better elections. Centralized state authority allows aggrieved citizens to hold a single entity accountable, either in court or at the polling place. The problem, however, is that localities—at least those with bipartisan election boards—may be more trustworthy with certain tasks. For example, a Democratic secretary of state's office may have more resources to maintain an accurate statewide voter-registration list. (The Help America Vote Act, by the way, requires the development of such a list.) If left unchecked, however, that Democratic secretary of state might employ an overinclusive computer program that, under the guise of "cleaning up" the list, disproportionately purges overseas military voters, who are more likely to vote Republican.

While these are difficult issues, Congress should still articulate minimum standards that states and localities must meet. The federal standards should not prescribe a single approach, but rather allow states to decide how to meet the standards. Two critical guidelines would require uniform procedures for counting ballots (including provisional ballots) and a minimum of one voting machine per 100 registered voters at a polling place.

"Sunshine" is also an important tool. Federal guidelines should prevent state and local officials from changing voting procedures without a public review process. Citizens would be able to comment on the design of a new butterfly ballot and shifts in polling-place machine distribution before the changes are implemented. Federal guidelines should also require that, after an election, states and localities publish democracy statements (not unlike a quarterly financial statement that a public company makes available for shareholders). Such statements should provide quantifiable post-election analysis of strengths and weaknesses of the adequacy and implementation not only of polling-place practices but also of pre–Election Day administrative functions such as voter purges and the processing of voter-registration forms. The statements should be crafted to allow county clerks and boards to observe trends, monitor progress, and anticipate problems before they occur, and they should be formatted so that one can easily assess how a particular county stacks up against all others in various categories.

Further, even as local and state officials run elections, the federal government should assume primary financial responsibility for elections, in order to ensure that every American casts a ballot at an adequately funded polling place. Existing incentives create significant disparities by compelling local politicians in less-wealthy municipalities to siphon money from elections toward such tangible goals as increasing student test scores and lowering crime rates. A CalTech/MIT study found that some counties spent only one-fifth of the amount per voter spent by other counties. While a few innovative low-spending counties may run better elections than high-spending counties, these spending disparities usually lead to inequality among voters in different localities.

The federal government should allocate a floor of funding to states and localities based on voting-age-citizen population (perhaps giving a bit more to smaller localities that cannot benefit from economies of scale). States and localities would use their discretion in spending the money, and the federal funds would not only preserve but also enhance responsible innovation that respects the rights of voters. Further, because the federal money would be earmarked for elections and could not be spent on other government services, less-wealthy localities no longer would have to choose whether to spend limited local tax dollars on democracy or on education.

Experts estimate that local governments spent approximately $1 billion on elections in 2000 (a presidential year). That may seem high, but it is not enough to ensure fair elections at the local level. A federal expenditure of $4 billion on elections every four years would double existing funds; this works out to an annual expense of less than one percent of the 2006 U.S. Department of Defense budget (0.24 percent, to be precise), or $5.17 per voting-age citizen. This would be higher than Great Britain's expenditure of $2.62 per voter but still much lower than Australia's $9.30 per voter. County and local tax money previously used on elections could be used to supplement federal election funds, diverted to further beef up local services such as schools and police, or returned to voters in the form of a tax cut. The point, however, is that all Americans would live in cities and counties that provided at least a basic level of election funding.[7]

In the preceding chapters, I've shown that politicians manipulate district boundaries and election rules to win elections, and their efforts are facilitated by a matrix of 4,600 different local election systems. Now that we've established that all voters are adversely affected by this system, I will explain how politicians use race to aquire and maintain power.

★　★　★　★　★　★　★　★　★　★　★　★　★　★

CHAPTER THREE

DOES RACE STILL MATTER?

I n December 2002, Republican Suzanne Haik Terrell had the
political opportunity of her life. A month earlier, the
Republicans had regained a majority in the United States Senate,
securing fifty-one seats out of 100. Conservatives across the nation
were now looking for Terrell to fortify the Republicans' slim majority by beating Louisiana's incumbent U.S. Senator, Democrat Mary
Landrieu, in a runoff election on December 7.

Terrell had the right stuff. The forty-eight-year-old Roman
Catholic had graduated from Tulane University and earned a law
degree from Loyola. She lived in New Orleans, thirteen houses
away from where she grew up. Images of Terrell's picture-perfect
physician husband and three daughters drove home a family-values
message. Two years earlier, she had won a race for state elections
commissioner and had become the first Republican woman elected
to statewide office in Louisiana.

A few days before the December 7 runoff election, pollsters proclaimed the race between Terrell and Landrieu a dead heat. One
poll showed Landrieu at 47 percent and Terrell at 45 percent, with
8 percent of voters undecided. "It is a toss-up," said pollster Brad

Coker, who noted that in most elections, undecided voters lean toward the challenger.

But Terrell, like many Republicans around the country, had a problem. Polls showed that although 58 percent of whites supported Terrell, only 6 percent of African Americans said they would vote for her. Other Republican candidates had invested time and money trying to attract black votes with little success. The best use of Terrell's finite resources seemed to be to win over undecided moderate white voters. She could only hope that fellow Republicans such as U.S. Senator Trent Lott of Mississippi would avoid race-tinged comments that might stimulate African-American turnout and alienate white moderates.

Terrell's Democratic opponent, Senator Mary Landrieu, was also an attractive candidate. Landrieu and her husband, Frank, an attorney, had two children. Perhaps most important, she had inherited a big name. Landrieu's father, Moon Landrieu, had been mayor of New Orleans and had served in President Jimmy Carter's cabinet. Two years after graduating from Louisiana State University, Mary Landrieu became the youngest woman ever elected to the Louisiana state legislature. In the U.S. Senate, she earned a reputation as a moderate Democrat who emphasized fiscal discipline.

Landrieu had a different race problem. Black Louisianans accounted for 32.5 percent of the state's population but made up only 26 percent of the electorate in the November 5 primary—the lowest in ten years. She could have avoided the entire runoff if she had secured a majority of the votes in the primary. Why didn't African Americans turn out for her?

Blacks had their reasons. Democratic State Senator Cleo Fields and many other African-American leaders claimed that Landrieu had failed to respond to the needs of their community. They resented her wooing of conservative white voters by boasting that she had voted with Republican President George W. Bush 74 percent of the time. "African-American voters should not be taken for granted by any elected official in a state that has such a high African-American population," Fields warned. (The political prospects of Landrieu and other Democrats would become even more complicated three years later when Hurricane Katrina's flooding of New Orleans prompted a mass exodus of black voters out of Louisiana.)

The polls for the December showdown shifted, depending on projections of black voter turnout. One poll, which showed Landrieu and Terrell tied if African Americans made up only 23 percent of the electorate, revealed that Landrieu would enjoy a six-point lead if black turnout reached 28 percent. A final poll—taken by Terrell's pollster, Verne Kennedy, the night before the election—showed that Terrell would win if African Americans made up only 26 percent of those who voted. "The higher it gets over 26 percent," said independent pollster Brad Coker, "the greater Landrieu's odds" of winning.

By noon on Election Day, it was clear that Landrieu might lose. Early reports showed turnout in African-American precincts to be lighter than expected. And Landrieu's opponents were on the attack. African-American youths held up signs in black neighborhoods parroting earlier statements by Democrat Cleo Fields: "Mary, if you don't respect us, don't expect us." The Louisiana Republican Party orchestrated and bankrolled the "grassroots" demonstration. They knew a soft spot when they saw one. Later, defending their actions, the GOP said merely that the signs accurately reflected the African-American community's frustration with Landrieu.

But other, less "accurate" postings had previously appeared. An unsigned flyer, distributed in African-American public-housing complexes in New Orleans just before the runoff election, claimed:

Vote!!! Bad Weather? No problem!!! If the weather is uncomfortable on election day (Saturday December 7th) Remember you can wait and cast your ballot on Tuesday December 10th.

There was no such rain date for voters to fall back on. The origins of this misleading flyer were never discovered.

The Landrieu campaign knew it was in big trouble. At 1 P.M., Louisiana native and former Al Gore campaign manager Donna Brazile set up a conference call with Landrieu, Cleo Fields, and former President Bill Clinton. One veteran political reporter said that "Brazile and Clinton were extremely blunt with Fields" in insisting that he immediately step up his get-out-the-vote operations in African-American neighborhoods in Baton Rouge. After the call, Landrieu raced to heavily black precincts in New Orleans with two popular African-American officials, Mayor Ray Nagin and Congressman William Jefferson. The trio and volunteers canvassed the community until the polls closed at 8 P.M. The Democratic phone banks did an all-out targeting of African-American neighborhoods from 6 to 8 P.M., urging residents to go out and vote.

The efforts worked. African-American turnout in Fields's district was 3.5 percent higher than in the November 5 primary. Statewide, the efforts by the Democrats pushed African-American turnout to 335,000—27.1 percent of the electorate. Summing up Landrieu's victory a week later, *Time* magazine reported: "[I]n the end, Landrieu managed to galvanize just enough of her crucial African-American base to break ahead."[1]

RACE AND POLITICS TODAY

Many claim that race has become a relatively insignificant factor in politics today. Edward Blum and Roger Clegg, leading critics of the Voting Rights Act, wrote: "[T]he voting habits of white Southerners, and nearly all white Americans, are today colorblind to an extent that only the wildest optimists would have envisioned in 1965." New York University Law Professor Samuel Issacharoff claims, "[N]o longer are blacks political outsiders," and "the Southern political process is highly attuned to black political claims."

Only a zealot would refuse to acknowledge that things have improved since the 1960s. The number of African-American elected officials jumped from about 200 in 1965 to 9,040 in 2000. The electoral successes of U.S. Senators Barack Obama and Carol Moseley Braun of Illinois, and Governors Bill Richardson of New Mexico, L. Douglas Wilder of Virginia, and Gary Locke of Washington state have established that certain candidates of color can win in the right political environment.

So, are these the good, new, color-blind days?

Color blindness may be politically correct, but it isn't politically accurate. As the Landrieu-Terrell contest in Louisiana shows, race is important largely because of the differences in voting patterns between whites and people of color. Across the nation, only 30 percent of whites are Democrats, but over 60 percent of African Americans are aligned with the party. Even independent African American voters trend Democratic; in 2004, for example, 88 percent of African-American voters cast a ballot for Democratic presidential nominee John Kerry. Latinos and Asian Americans lean Democratic, although they are not as reliable as African Americans. Similarly, on social issues such as affirmative action and the role of the government in ensuring equal opportunity and integration, people of color as a group are much more liberal than whites.

And these differences do not merely stem from racial disparities in class. On average, people of color and whites of the same socioeconomic status have vastly different political preferences. Rather than getting narrower over time, the racial differences in political perspective in many areas are more significant than they were twenty years ago.

Due to different voting patterns, racial turnout determines election outcomes throughout the United States. The following are some recent examples of race swinging the election:

Nevada, 1998. An aggressive get-out-the-vote effort nearly doubled Latino participation compared with 1996 numbers, allowing Democrat Harry Reid to win a U.S. Senate seat by 379 votes. (In 2004, Reid became the Democratic leader in the U.S. Senate.)

Mississippi, 2003. Former National Republican Party Chair Haley Barbour beat incumbent Democratic Governor Ronnie Musgrove by fewer than 61,000 votes. African Americans, who make up more than a third of the state's population, cast 94 percent of their votes for Musgrove, but their turnout was not large enough to offset the 77 percent of white voters who favored Barbour. By emphasizing Governor Musgrove's opposition to the Confederate insignia on Mississippi's state flag, Barbour attracted 115,000 new voters to the polls; four out of five of them cast their ballots for the Republican.

Washington, 2004. In a governor's race that saw two recounts and several trips to the state supreme court, Democrat Christine Gregoire was finally certified the winner over Republican Dino Rossi two months after Election Day. Her winning margin was a mere 128 votes out of more than 2.9 million cast. Most Asian Americans voted for Gregoire. Seventy percent in the state turned out to vote, whereas only 57 percent of Asian Americans went to the polls. No recounts would have been necessary had the turnout rate among Asian Americans and whites been identical.

In political contests between candidates of different ethnicities, polarized voting is even more stark. In the 1990s, two-thirds of Southern whites voted for the white congressional candidate over the black one. And it is not that these voters were casting ballots only for Republicans. White Democratic candidates enjoyed about a ten-point advantage over black Democratic candidates in attracting white votes. Voters of color were even more cohesive, with blacks casting about 93 percent of their votes for the African-American congressional candidate. Studies of other races have shown that many Latino voters also show a preference for Hispanic candidates. As mentioned in chapter 1, for example, three of four Latinos voted for Latino challenger Raul Godinez over white incumbent Howard Berman in their 1998 California Democratic primary contest for Congress. Much has been made of the fact that racially polarized voting is on the decline, but in places such as Charleston, South Carolina, whites in recent years have been less likely to vote for African-American candidates than in earlier decades.

Throughout the United States, political contests featuring candidates of different ethnicities have sparked racial bloc voting:

Houston, 2001. Incumbent Democrat Lee Brown, the city's first African-American mayor, increased African-American turnout by 30 percent to narrowly defeat Republican Orlando Sanchez by one percentage point. Latino turnout was double the number in 1997—and Sanchez received 72 percent of Latino votes.

Milwaukee, 2004. In a nonpartisan mayoral race featuring two Democrats, white candidate Tom Barrett beat African-American candidate Marvin Pratt. Half of the city's residents are white, and more than a third are African American. Polls showed that 83 percent of white voters preferred Barrett, and 92 percent of African-American voters cast ballots for Pratt.

Louisiana, 2003. Whites who had voted against Democrat Mary Landrieu for U.S. Senate in 2002 switched over a year later and voted for Democrat Kathleen Blanco for governor. In the twenty-six parishes that had favored former Ku Klux Klan leader David Duke in a prior election, Blanco averaged ten percentage points higher than Landrieu. How did things improve so quickly for the second white female Democrat? Ms. Landrieu faced a white opponent—Republican Suzanne Haik Terrell—while Ms. Blanco ran against Bobby Jindal, a conservative Republican of South Asian descent. Pollsters put Jindal ten points ahead of Blanco four days before the 2003 gubernatorial election, but the Republican lost by four points. One last-minute Blanco television ad proclaimed,

"Wake Up, Louisiana! Before It's Too Late!" and featured a photograph of a young, dark-skinned Jindal with his hair sticking up. "If Jindal had been white, he'd be governor right now," said Lance Hill, head of the Southern Institute for Education and Research, a race-relations institute based at Tulane University.[2]

HANGING ON TO POWER

The problem of race in politics is not simply that voters cast ballots along racial lines. Voters of all races—including those with unpopular views like Ku Klux Klan sympathizers—should have the freedom to band together to participate in democracy and advocate their views. While I'm not endorsing racial factions among Louisiana Republicans or Milwaukee Democrats, the primary threat to democracy is not voters. Instead, it is political operatives who continue to win elections by manipulating election rules to doctor racial turnout.

Kilmichael, Mississippi, 2001. The number of African Americans in Kilmichael had grown to over 52 percent of the town's population. The mayor and all five members of the board of aldermen were white, however, and only one African American had ever been elected to the board. Prior to the June 2001 general election, several African-American candidates qualified for the mayoral and board races, and there was a very strong possibility that African-American candidates would win most of the municipal offices. Three weeks before the general election, however, the incumbent board of aldermen voted unanimously to cancel the election. The board's stated purpose was to change Kilmichael's townwide system for electing town officials to districts.

Ville Platte, Louisiana, 2003. The African-American population in Ville Platte jumped from about 25 percent of the town's population in 1980 to 56.6 percent in 2000. In 2003, city officials proposed a redistricting plan that reduced the African-American population in one of its six council districts from 55.1 to 38.1 percent, shifting many African Americans within this district to another that was already 78.8 percent African American. The shift effectively reduced the number of predominantly African-American council districts from four to three.

Town of North, South Carolina, 2003. In the early 1990s, a number of African Americans who lived southeast of the town's current boundary petitioned to become a part of North. African Americans would have become a majority of the town's population if officials accepted the petition. With no explanation, town officials denied the application. In September 2003, however, the town of North approved a petition to annex a small group of whites into their town.

In none of these examples did politicians employ billy clubs, fire hoses, tear gas, or police dogs to prevent people of color from casting a vote. But we don't need a twenty-first-century white sheriff attacking voters of color on national television in order to ask questions about race. Eliminating the doctoring of election procedures by state and local political operatives, rather than restraining troopers who inflict state-sponsored violence to prevent blacks from voting, is today's challenge.

To be sure, some would say that politics, not race, motivates many practices that exclude voters of color. For example, perhaps opponents of Mary Landrieu in New Orleans distributed misleading voting information in black neighborhoods not out of racial animus but because they wanted their candidate, Suzanne Haik Terrell, to win. Perhaps the white elected officials in Kilmichael, Mississippi, canceled the June 2001 election because they wanted to hang onto their seats, and would have taken the same action if confronted by a group of white voters likely to vote against them.

I can't sidestep the issue of race versus politics. If today's ethnicity is based not just on skin color but also on political perspective, why does the exclusion of Latino voters raise more concern than the exclusion of Texas Democrats? Why is racial exclusion different from shutting out voters based on other factors, such as political party affiliation, class, or religion?

RACE OR POLITICS?

The only reason many Americans might have heard of Bayou La Batre, Alabama, is that it is the home of the fictional character Forrest Gump, portrayed by actor Tom Hanks in the 1994 feature film bearing the same name. In reality, the rural town sits on the Gulf Coast and has been hit by a downturn in the shrimp industry. About a quarter of the boats in the community's 120-to-130-vessel shrimping fleet have been repossessed for nonpayment, and $100,000 in federal assistance was distributed to help shrimpers pay their electric bills. A local doctor accepts "fresh-caught crab, homemade pies, and handpicked vegetables" as payment because, she says, "Most folks in this community are too poor to afford medical care but too rich to qualify for Medicaid." (In 2005, Hurricane Katrina would make matters even worse in Bayou La Batre. The storm sank or capsized 80 percent of the town's shrimp fleet and destroyed or left uninhabitable 800 homes.)

While the Alabama town of 2,700 maintains a majority white population, a recent influx of Vietnamese, Laotian, and Cambodian immigrants has changed Bayou La Batre's complexion. By 2004, residents of Asian ancestry accounted for one-third of the population. Despite their significant presence, for many years Asian Americans did not participate in the political process. Of more than 800 votes cast in the 1996 town elections, for example, only about fifteen were cast by Asian-American residents.

Several years ago, an area realtor, noting the trend of longtime residents moving out of town, told a reporter, "People don't put up a billboard and announce they are leaving because of immigrants, but you can tell what's on their mind." A former mayor, Warren Seaman, said, "There are only one or two [Asian-Americans] in the community I can talk to. The rest are standoffish." Still, he acknowledged, "They represent a third of our community and they need representation on our council."

In August 2004, Phuong Tan Huynh, age thirty-three, ran to become the first Asian-American councilman in Bayou La Batre. He had lived in the town for more than two decades. When he was a child, Huynh's family had moved from a refugee camp in Vietnam to the United States and ultimately settled in Bayou La Batre. "I've been drilling it in their [Asian-Americans'] heads for a few years now that they could be the deciding factor in city elections," Fred Marceaux, who serves as an adviser to the local Asian-American community, told the *Mobile Register* newspaper. "I think some of them finally took it to heart."

Huynh's opponent was J. E. "Jackie" Ladnier, a white Alabama native. Under state law, a campaign may challenge the qualifications of any voter. As Asian Americans entered the polling place at the Bayou La Batre Community Center, they were approached by Ladnier and his supporters. Ladnier, denying racism, explained his strategy: "A lot of them, we didn't know but had to make a judgment, say, if someone came and met them outside then led them inside and seemed to be guiding them through it. Also, we figured if they couldn't speak good English, they possibly weren't American citizens." Huynh's sister, Linh Huynh Tran, had another perspective: "These people were just hoping that if they challenged our voters, they would just back out. They'd feel like they were in some kind of trouble or they'd be intimidated by all the paperwork in English."

One of the voters challenged by Ladnier's campaign, eighty-three-year-old Truong Tran, said through a translator, "It's hard for me to get out and walk as it is. . . . But I got out to vote because people told me it would take two or three minutes." Rather than joining other voters to cast a ballot quickly on the electronic machines, however, Mr. Tran was directed to a separate area and instructed to fill out a paper challenge ballot. At the time, Mr. Tran had been a Bayou La Batre resident for sixteen years and a U.S. citizen for eight years.

Phuong Tan Huynh eventually won a council seat by fewer than 100 votes.

Let's assume, just for the sake of conversation, that Ladnier challenged the voters for the very same reason Huynh worked to turn out the Asian-American vote: Both surmised that most voters of Asian descent would cast a ballot for Huynh. Ladnier's interest in challenging a large number of voters who appeared to be of Asian descent was motivated not by racial hatred but by his desire to prevent his political opponent from collecting illegitimate, and perhaps even legitimate, votes. Imagine that the following thoughts were flowing through the heads of Ladnier and his political supporters:

> Welcome to the big game. In a rough-and-tumble political world in which the pros from all parties hit hard with misleading negative campaign ads and titillating leaks about an opponent's extramarital affairs, challenging voters prone to vote against you is par for the course. Racially targeted challenges are akin to attempts to gerrymander congressional districts to diminish the strength of voters of an opposing political party, or attempts by Democrats or minority candidates to mobilize minority voters to go to the polls. Why should people of color who tend to vote in a particular way be off-limits in politics? Such an exception is itself paternalistically racist.

Ladnier's actions are not problematic, he might claim, because his acts constitute political discrimination rather than racial discrimination. Is Ladnier right? Is it OK if the motivation is political gain rather than racial hatred?

Almost everyone struggles with the intersection of race and politics—including the U.S. Supreme Court. In the 1993 case *Shaw v. Reno*, for example, the Court criticized "bizarrely drawn" predominantly African-American districts and wrote that a constitutional violation could occur if race, rather than politics, was the "predominant factor" in drawing a district. The justices envisioned race and politics as two different things and determined that political gerrymandering is fine but racial gerrymandering is questionable. In 2001, the civil-rights community flipped the script when it persuaded the Court in *Easley v. Cromartie* that the unique Democratic political philosophy of most African Americans—rather than "race"—was the predominant factor that motivated the drawing of another predominantly African-American district in North Carolina. The law on race and politics remains unsettled.

When traditional civil-rights advocates confront the intersection of race and politics, they often choose to emphasize race and underplay political motive. Their tactic is understandable. Conservatives already label civil-rights groups as "liberal fronts" that covertly support Democratic candidates and progressive issues, and an acknowledgment of political motives threatens to give credence to those claims. Similarly, highlighting that political operatives often suppress African-American votes to undermine Democratic prospects might evoke little sympathy from a Republican-controlled Congress. Examining the relationship between race and politics might also undermine the moral power of civil-rights imagery established in the 1960s that continues to sustain public support for civil-rights protections. If race is the elephant in the room that conservatives refuse to acknowledge, politics is the key issue that many civil-rights advocates have so far ignored.

But civil-rights advocates cannot continue to defend prior gains without squarely facing politics. The highly publicized O.J.

Simpson trial fortified a "race card" lexicon that shapes public opinion. Many Americans presume that those who discuss race do so not to correct racial injustice but to advance a self-serving motive. According to conventional wisdom, O.J. Simpson's lawyers portrayed detective Mark Fuhrman as a racist so that O.J. could escape a penalty for having murdered his former wife and her friend. This phenomenon carries over to politics. Democrats, the argument goes, label Republicans as Jim Crow–era vote suppressors in order to stimulate African-American voting and to try to villainize Republican candidates in the eyes of white swing voters. But charges of both politics and race may be at work. O.J. could be guilty and Mark Fuhrman might be a racist. Democratic claims of voter suppression might be motivated by party operatives' political interests, yet some Republicans might target black voters for suppression. But due to the emergence of the "race card" phenomenon, many Americans summarily dismiss a reference to race, and thus civil-rights advocates cannot rely solely on caricatures like Bull Connor to preserve civil-rights protections. A frank, contemporary discussion of the relationship between race and politics is needed.

Rather than insisting that most political operatives of the twenty-first century are "racists" in the tradition of the Ku Klux Klan, civil-rights advocates need to grapple with a thornier series of questions that confront us now. If whites and people of color have different preferences—and if political operatives attempt to suppress voters of color—to what extent should this be viewed as just "dirty politics" or as something more threatening to democracy? Politicians use a variety of criteria to categorize voters: race, gender, religion, residence, socioeconomic status, party affiliation, and past support for particular candidates. What makes race worthy of special protection on that list? Why aren't racial groups just like other special-interest groups?

Perhaps U.S. Supreme Court Justice John Paul Stevens best

articulated the claim that neither race nor politics should be used to disenfranchise voters. Justice Stevens argued that politicians disenfranchise identifiable groups of voters prone to cast ballots against them, and regardless of whether those voters can be identified as part of religious, political, economic, or racial groups, they all deserve protection. According to Justice Stevens, any interpretation that the Constitution is particularly concerned about political exclusion of African Americans or Latinos while tolerating exclusion of other identifiable groups organized along religious, economic, or political lines "would be inconsistent with the basic tenet of the Equal Protection Clause."[3]

I can't think of a principled reason why it is moral to suppress the votes of Republicans, Jews, or blind Americans but immoral to suppress African-American, Latino, or Asian-American votes. Such a distinction erroneously suggests that a vote cast by a person of color is worth more than a vote cast by a white American.

RACE AS THE STARTING POINT IN VOTER PROTECTION

Even though the votes of people of color are not worth more than those of individuals in religious, political, or other types of groups, the law should still make efforts to prevent suppression targeted at people of color. Just as a local police force directs rape-prevention information toward women—even though a woman's bodily integrity is no more valuable than that of a man—particular traits of race justify concentrated efforts to prevent suppression of voters of color. Physical appearance, socioeconomic factors such as housing segregation, and distinct voting trends make people of color particularly vulnerable targets for exclusion.[4]

I could go down a conventional liberal path to give race a special status, focusing on past wrongs. I could write pages about how discriminatory immigration laws—such as the 1882 Chinese Exclusion Act and the Immigration Act of 1924—purposely shaped the racial composition of our nation so that even today people of color are a numerical minority. Any such lecture would note that our racial history—including the Civil War—continues to shape the political identity of Americans of all racial backgrounds and explains the large numbers of upper-class black Democrats and working-class white Republicans. Ignoring this history, the argument goes, gives license to today's political operatives to exclude voters of color to win elections and perpetuate racial inequality. White supremacy is the original sin of America, the soliloquy might point out, and, like a recovering alcoholic, our nation needs to bend over backward to avoid falling into old habits.

I have friends who are tired of these arguments; their eyes glaze over. They feel as though each day the history of white supremacy is further away from our present reality. While these friends might acknowledge history, to them the past doesn't fully explain why the law should make a special effort to prevent political manipulation of voters of color today. Therefore, rather than invoking history to try to garner either sympathy or a political reparation owed to people of color, I will tell a story to explain what can happen in the future if we tolerate racial suppression today. Earlier politicians used partisan advantage rather than racial animus to justify suppression of voters of color, but the political exclusion itself fueled racial hostility.

In the early 1800s, blacks in New York state voted solidly for the Federalist Party and against the Democratic-Republican Party (which became the Democratic Party in the 1820s). As a result, Democrats consistently worked to suppress the black vote. Democratic operatives challenged the qualifications of black voters at the polls (assuming they were runaway slaves rather than freedmen), and the Federalists objected to this practice. State

Assemblyman Erastus Root had abolitionist leanings, yet his partisan affiliation with Democrats prompted him to support black disenfranchisement. Commenting on a particularly close election, Root noted: "[T]he votes of three hundred Negroes in the city of New York, in 1813, decided the election in favor of the Federal party, and also decided the political character of the legislature of this state." The Federalists soon lost their majority, and the new political powers adopted elaborate registration requirements for blacks, requiring that they always "bring full copies of such registration to the officers of the election." By 1826, a Democratic-controlled legislature erased for white males the qualifications that voters own land worth at least $250 and pay taxes, but it maintained the requirements for blacks.

Twenty years later, during the 1846 state constitutional convention, the committee chair, former Governor William C. Bouck, proposed limiting suffrage to white men, and the Whigs moved to strike the word *white*. (As successors to the Federalist Party, the Whigs also enjoyed overwhelming black support.) The convention voted 63–37 against racial equality. The votes came down largely along partisan lines, with four out of five Whigs voting for equality and nineteen of every twenty Democrats voting to deny blacks the franchise. When the provision was referred to the populace for ratification, "Whig counties followed the direction of their leaders, and Democratic counties did the same," wrote Columbia University Professor Dixon Ryan Fox in 1917. Even Democratic counties with strong abolitionist leanings voted against equality for blacks. "It was a party matter in which personalities or the fortunes of slavery in southern states or in the territories had but little bearing."[5]

Race is relevant today for the same reasons it was relevant in nineteenth-century New York. The different voting patterns of many people of color give politicians the motive to suppress their votes, and the unique physical and socioeconomic traits that characterize people of color make them particularly vulnerable.

Race is often an observable characteristic, as was evident in Bayou La Batre in 2004. The physical aspect of race allowed someone like Jackie Ladnier to readily identify and target voters whom he believed would vote against him and for Phuong Tan Huynh.

Socioeconomic factors such as housing segregation and racial disparities in wealth, educational attainment, incarceration, and English proficiency also make people of color easy targets for political shenanigans. For example, a 2002 study showed that the median net worth of white households was more than ten times higher than both African-American and Latino households. Latinos are twice as likely as whites to be incarcerated, and blacks are six times as likely as whites to be incarcerated. Nearly half of all Asian-language and Spanish speakers in the United States speak English less than "very well," compared with about 8 percent of the total U.S. population.[6] These factors make today's voters of color—in the aggregate—particularly susceptible to doctored election districts, poll challenges, punch-card machines, lifetime felon-disenfranchisement rules, and English-only ballots.

Because race is inherited, the damage done by voter suppression along racial lines is particularly daunting. Excluding a racial group from the political process not only can silence a political perspective in a particular election cycle, but also can result in government policies such as segregated schools and home-ownership programs that affect a racial community for generations.

Race also warrants attention because rapidly expanding Asian-American and Latino populations pose a threat to incumbent politicians vested in the status quo. In California, whites remain the largest racial group but no longer make up a majority of the state's population. California Common Cause Executive Director Kathay Feng tells of incumbents in her state who claimed their districts contained "too many Asians" and—nervous about Asian-American challengers—had their districts redrawn to reduce Asian-American vote totals. As mentioned in chapter 1, the Mexican

American Legal Defense and Educational Fund sued over similar gerrymandering that reduced Latino vote totals. Demographic trends suggest incumbents in other states will soon be tempted to adopt this strategy. Between 1990 and 2000, the Latino population quadrupled in Southern states such as Arkansas, North Carolina, and Tennessee. By 2050, whites are expected to fall from 70 percent of the U.S. population to 49.6 percent, and Latino and Asian-American populations are expected to double. Ten million new Latinos and Asian Americans are expected to join the voting rolls over the next fifteen years, and we need to ensure that incumbents do not manipulate the matrix to diminish participation by these new voters.[7]

Rather than giving people of color "special rights," acknowledging and dismantling barriers faced by racial groups produces benefits for voters of many other backgrounds. Poor whites, for example, are more likely to be hindered by lifetime felon-disenfranchisement laws than wealthier whites. Outdated punch-card machines produce more spoiled ballots in predominantly African-American precincts than in white ones, but by adopting better technology, voters of all races will cast ballots that are more likely to be counted. Redesigning the matrix to include people of color opens democracy to millions of other Americans.[8]

SUPPRESSION VERSUS MOBILIZATION

If race should not be used as a tool of political exclusion, why should it be used as a tool to *include* voters? Why should Jackie Ladnier be banned from using race as a tool to identify his likely opponents while Phuong Tan Huynh can use it to mobilize his supporters? Why scrutinize Republican attempts to suppress African-American votes and tolerate Democratic targeting of African-American neighborhoods for get-out-the-vote efforts? A desire to win elections, rather than to empower voters, probably motivates voter-mobilization efforts by the Democrats, and perhaps to some extent candidates like Huynh.

But voter suppression and voter mobilization are fundamentally opposing objectives. First of all, mobilization of voters stimulates voter autonomy and choice. Voters can either choose to stay home or go to the polls and vote Democratic or Republican. Just as voting empowers individual voters, so does mobilization. Those who have not been mobilized are not harmed by targeted mobilization. Whites who are not mobilized by Democrats, for example, are not being denied access. Suppression, on the other hand, reduces voter autonomy by denying the voter a choice. Even when we disagree with the views of those mobilized—progressives, for example, often disdain the use of wedge issues such as the Confederate flag or gay marriage to mobilize Republican voters—mobilization furthers democracy and suppression is antidemocratic.

Second, mobilization of people of color enhances fairness and equality in representation because studies show that wealthier, better-educated whites are the most likely group to vote. Granted, one might claim that mobilization distorts results because "'slackers' should not decide elections."[9] But government should represent *all* of the people, and mobilization of people of color helps ensure that elections reflect the views of a diverse group of voters. On the other hand, suppression of voters of color, who are already underrepresented in the political process, systematically distorts democracy and makes it more likely that government will disregard the needs and priorities of those excluded.

Political operatives of all stripes attempt to engineer racial turnout (either up or down) to win elections. We could minimize this, and ensure that government policy better reflects the population as a whole, by requiring all citizens to vote, as Australia does.

But such a law will probably not be on the books in the United States anytime soon. In light of our current system, we should recognize that suppression and mobilization differ, and we should make special efforts to prevent suppression.

THE LIMITS OF RACE

Although racial suppression poses unique dangers, race should be used carefully. For example, the law should not tolerate a double standard in which Huynh's supporters can target white voters at the polls for challenges while Ladnier's supporters can't engage in a similar practice against Asian-American voters. We should not conclude that as the party of "blacks," Democrats are entitled to a particular quota of seats in a state legislature, or that party leaders have a free pass to manipulate black populations within districts while Republicans are barred from similar activity.

But even though there must be limits to the matter of race, it is illogical to ignore the correlation between race and politics and profess that they exist in two artificial and distinct boxes—racial animus and dirty but tolerable politics. These separate racial and political paradigms give us a structure within which to analyze problems. The problem, however, is that these oversimplified approaches do not accurately describe the bulk of challenges we face today that do not fit neatly into either category. Our current discussion of race and politics is counterproductive in that it encourages civil-rights advocates to attempt to prove that political strategists are "racists" in order to justify the continued existence of voting-rights protections. It also prompts conventionally labeled political "opponents" of racial communities to dismiss real harms that stem from exclusion along racial lines.

Practices that suppress voters of color, even when undertaken or tolerated for partisan purposes, facilitate racial inequality. By consciously ensuring that election rules do not intentionally or inadvertently exclude voters of color, we encourage democratic engagement and racial reconciliation that benefits the entire nation.

As the next chapter will show, however, a primary tool for racial inclusion—the Voting Rights Act—is currently under attack.

★ ★ ★ ★ ★ ★ ★ ★ ★ ★ ★ ★ ★ ★ ★

CHAPTER FOUR

NO BACKSLIDING

A month after Republican Abraham Lincoln's victory in the November 1860 presidential election, South Carolina seceded from the United States. In the document that effectively became the first Declaration of Independence of the Confederate States of America, South Carolina officials wrote:

> . . . A geographical line has been drawn across the Union, and all the States north of that line have united in the election of a man to the high office of President of the United States, whose opinions and purposes are hostile to slavery. . . . [Lincoln's election] has been aided in some of the States by elevating to citizenship, persons who . . . are incapable of becoming citizens; and their votes have been used to inaugurate a new policy, hostile to the South, and destructive of its beliefs and safety.

> [On March 4, Lincoln's Republicans] will take possession of the Government. . . . The slaveholding States will no longer have the power of self-government, or self-protection, and the Federal Government will have become their enemy. . . . We, therefore, the People of South Carolina . . . have solemnly declared that the

Union heretofore existing between this State and the other States
of North America, is dissolved. . . .

Four years and more than 500,000 American deaths later,
Confederate General Robert E. Lee surrendered on April 9, 1865,
at Appomattox Court House in Virginia. Five days after Lee's sur-
render, Confederate sympathizer John Wilkes Booth assassinated
Republican President Abraham Lincoln at the Ford Theatre in
Washington, DC. Vice President Andrew Johnson was sworn in as
commander-in-chief in the hours following Lincoln's death.

That summer, former Confederates began to regain power in the
Southern states. Although Lincoln's Emancipation Proclamation
had freed slaves in Confederate states two years earlier, white
Democrats enacted "Black Codes" that prohibited blacks from voting, mandated black employment, and reestablished other features
of the old slave system. The Radical Republicans in Congress
believed Johnson—himself a Tennessee Democrat originally
tapped as Lincoln's running mate to promote national unity—was
too tolerant of the former Confederates' power grab.

Over Johnson's veto, a Republican-controlled Congress passed
the Reconstruction Act in March 1867. The act deemed the governments in ten former Confederate states illegal and divided them
into five districts to be governed by military generals. Occupying
federal troops were to oversee voter registration, and adult males
of all races would be entitled to vote, except for many Southern
white military officers and political officeholders who had broken
their oath to defend the U.S. Constitution by siding with the
Confederacy. Since most freed African Americans were
Republicans and most Southern whites were Democrats, the provisions bolstered the Republicans' political power.

The Reconstruction Act also mandated that eligible voters in
former Confederate states convene state constitutional conven-

tions, and that each new state constitution guarantee blacks the right to vote. African-American voting rights were further solidified by ratification of the Fifteenth Amendment to the U.S. Constitution in 1870, which prohibited the denial of the right to vote on account of race.

These federal protections allowed voters to elect several blacks to become delegates to state constitutional conventions, and later state legislators and congressmen. Between 1870 and 1900, Southern states sent 700 African Americans to state legislatures and 22 African Americans to Congress. (Between 1970 and 2000, these states sent 23 African Americans to Congress.) In South Carolina, blacks held 69 percent of the seats in the state legislature, and Jonathan Jasper Wright sat as a justice on the state supreme court. Blacks in other states had big jobs as well: Hiram R. Revels and Blanche Kelso Bruce represented Mississippi in the U.S. Senate, and P. B. S. Pinchback served as acting governor of Louisiana. Northern white Republicans—labeled "carpetbaggers" because many moved to the south carrying their possessions in bags made of carpeting—assumed important administrative positions throughout the South. Other government posts were given to "scalawags," native white Southern politicians who joined the Republican Party, worked with blacks, and were perceived as opportunistic turncoats by most white Southerners.

The domination of Republicans—largely freed slaves assisted by white carpetbaggers and scalawags—inflamed white Democrats. White Southerners struck back by forming groups like the Ku Klux Klan to prevent voting by blacks. The Klan tortured and lynched African Americans who tried to vote, and by 1870 their terrorism helped to reestablish white Democratic rule in Georgia, North Carolina, and Tennessee. In May 1872, Congress passed the Amnesty Act, which restored voting rights to most Confederate sympathizers. Two years later, the Democrats regained domination of the U.S. House of Representatives; by 1876, Republicans controlled state governments in only three of the eleven former Confederate states.

The tension was thick in the weeks following the 1876 presidential election. Democrat Samuel J. Tilden, governor of New York, faced Republican Rutherford B. Hayes, governor of Ohio. Tilden led by nineteen votes in the electoral college, but accusations of failure to count ballots by Republican election boards in South Carolina, Florida, and Louisiana left the nation in limbo. Republicans responded that they merely discarded returns in areas where white Democrats prevented African Americans from voting. When a recount failed to resolve the conflict, Congress created a special electoral commission comprising eight Republicans and seven Democrats.

A few days before the March 1877 inauguration ceremonies, politicians on the commission reached a deal. The Democrats would give the presidency to Republican Hayes, and the Republicans would agree to withdraw federal soldiers from the South and effectively end Reconstruction.

In the absence of federal intervention, the backsliding began. Southern white Democrats created voting regulations that denied most blacks the right to vote without explicitly mentioning race. Poll taxes, literacy tests, and other devices cleared the voter rolls of blacks, most of whom were Republican. Violence took care of those few blacks who dared to attempt to vote despite the regulations.

Poll taxes required that voters pay a $1 or $2 fee to vote, which few newly freed slaves could afford. Adjusted for inflation, a $2 poll tax in 1880 would equal more than $35 today. Even accounting for inflation, people earned much less in 1880, and $2 represented at least two weeks' salary for most Americans. The poll tax also fortified Democratic Party rule by disenfranchising poor whites, many of whom were Populists (an emerging but ultimately unsuccessful third-party movement that Democrats criticized for attempting to unite whites and blacks). The Alabama poll tax, for example, disenfranchised approximately 25 percent of the white men in the state.

County registrars also required that citizens pass literacy or interpretation tests before being added to the registration rolls. Before emancipation, slaves were prohibited by law from learning to read, and most were uneducated and illiterate. Registrars often exercised discretion in administering these tests. Louisiana's interpretation test, for example, allowed registrars to demand that prospective voters demonstrate a knowledge of the state constitution, and the registrars themselves determined whether an answer was correct. Regarding a provision of the constitution, "FRDUM FOOF SPETGH" was considered an acceptable response from one white voter. But an African American was rejected for interpreting "people have the right peaceably to assemble" as meaning that "one may assemble or belong to any group, club or organization he chooses as long as it is within the law."

The results were drastic. While a majority of adult black males in all but two Southern states voted in the 1880 presidential election, virtually all had been eliminated from the voter rolls 1910. In Louisiana, the 1888 voter-registration rolls contained the names of 127,923 African Americans and 126,884 whites. By 1910, only 730 African Americans remained registered. United States Senator Ben "Pitchfork" Tillman of South Carolina, a white Democrat, boasted of black disenfranchisement in his state: "We have done our level best. We have scratched our heads to find out how we could eliminate every last one of them. We stuffed ballot boxes. We shot them. We are not ashamed of it."

This assault on black voters emptied Congress and state legislatures of black elected officials. While twenty-two African Americans served in Congress in the aftermath of the Civil War, by 1896 Representative George White of North Carolina was the only one left. After White retired in 1901, it would be another seventy-one years before the South would elect an African American to the U.S. Congress.

For the next six decades, African Americans were almost completely shut out of politics in the South, and segregation reigned. Blacks across the nation started to drift from the Republican Party to the Democratic Party during Franklin Roosevelt's administration, but Southern white Democrats' continued exclusion of blacks allowed them to maintain segregation and direct the bulk of public funds to white schools, parks, and other public facilities. Even though blacks had the right to vote under the Fifteenth Amendment, it was not effectively enforced. Whenever civil-rights lawyers would successfully challenge a discriminatory voting practice in court, the locality sued would simply replace its old practice with a new one that had the same effect of excluding blacks.

Politics in Selma, Alabama—the largest city in Dallas County— illustrated this problem. By the early 1960s, Dallas County had a voting-age population estimated at 29,500, just over half of whom were black. But the county's registration rolls included roughly two-thirds of the county's white residents and only one percent of its black residents. White politicians held all elected positions and maintained their power by requiring that applicants for registration pass an oral exam about the U.S. Constitution and possess "good character."

Justice Department lawyers had filed a lawsuit against the Dallas County registrars in 1961; after thirteen months of procedural wrangling, the case came to trial. By that time, the county registrars had resigned and the trial judge refused to ban tests because the new county registrars had not yet discriminated against blacks. After an appeal, federal courts finally ordered county registrars to stop requiring voters to interpret the *federal* constitution. At that point, the county registrars simply added a new test that required voters to demonstrate an "understanding" of the *state* constitution. After additional legal filings by the Justice Department, federal courts finally banned the new test. Yet, during the four years the lawsuit was working its way through the courts, only 383 of the 15,000 eligible black citizens registered.

In early 1965, John Lewis, a twenty-five-year-old African-American leader of the Student Nonviolent Coordinating Committee (SNCC), led his group to Dallas County. On March 7, Lewis and a group of 600—including teachers, teens, beauticians, and shopkeepers—began their protest march from Selma to the state capital of Montgomery, fifty miles away. They made it only six blocks, reaching the top of the crest of the Edmund Pettus Bridge, before Lewis stopped in his tracks. He remembers what he saw:

> There, facing us at the bottom of the other side, stood a sea of blue-helmeted, blue-uniformed Alabama state troopers, line after line of them, dozens of battle-ready lawmen stretched from one side of U.S. Highway 80 to the other.
>
> Behind them were several dozen more armed men—Sheriff [Jim] Clark's posse—some on horseback, all wearing khaki clothing, many carrying clubs the size of baseball bats.
>
> On one side of the road I could see a crowd of about a hundred whites, laughing and hollering, waving Confederate flags.

As the marchers moved forward silently, troopers pulled on their gas masks. When the marchers reached the bottom of the bridge, they stopped. After ordering the nonviolent marchers to disperse, the troopers rushed forward, shooting canisters of tear gas, trampling marchers with horses, and pummeling them with nightsticks and whips. "[O]ne posseman had a rubber hose wrapped with barbed wire," Lewis remembers. Even as the marchers scrambled back across the bridge, mounted and unmounted troopers went after them, attacking anyone who was in the street.

"I thought I was going to die," recalls Lewis, who was struck in the head and knocked unconscious. Doctors later diagnosed a fractured skull. Another ninety demonstrators suffered an assortment of injuries, which included open head gashes and broken arms, legs, ribs, jaws, and teeth.

That night, the ABC television network interrupted its Sunday-night movie, *Judgment at Nuremberg*—a 1961 film about Nazi Germany—to show gruesome images of peaceful protesters in America bleeding, vomiting, and crying out in agony at the hands of an army of white troopers.

The conflict, which became known as "Bloody Sunday," shocked America and sparked a public outcry. Demonstrators organized protests in more than eighty cities denouncing the violence, and sympathizers poured into Alabama from across the nation. Eight days later, Democratic President Lyndon Johnson appeared on national television to call for the passage of a new voting-rights law. "There is no Negro problem. There is no Southern problem. There is no Northern problem. There is only an American problem," Johnson said. "And we *shall* overcome."[1]

Five months later, President Johnson signed the Voting Rights Act of 1965.

THE VOTING RIGHTS ACT

The act suspended literacy and interpretation tests for voters and provided federal officials to register black voters and monitor local elections in the South. Perhaps the most important part of the act, however, was the Section 5 preclearance provision.

Section 5 required that a state or locality obtain approval ("preclearance") from the federal government whenever it wanted to change its election law. The goal was to prevent an area stripped of one discriminatory tool from backsliding by simply adopting a different exclusionary device. The preclearance requirement only applied to areas that had devices such as literacy tests and low voter turnout—initially Alabama, Alaska, Georgia, Louisiana, Mississippi, South Carolina, Virginia, and certain counties in Arizona, Hawaii, Idaho, and North Carolina.

Here's a relatively recent example of how the law works. In August 1999, the Board of Supervisors in Dinwiddie County, Virginia, voted to move the polling place in the Darvills Precinct from the Cut Bank Hunt Club to the Bott Memorial Church. Dinwiddie County is rural, with a voting-age population of just under 19,000. It sits twenty-five miles south of Richmond and describes itself as "noted for its rich Civil War history." The county is just under two-thirds white and more than one-third African American. The Darvills Precinct is particularly rural, has no incorporated towns or public schools, and stretches twelve miles from west to east. Soon after the Board of Supervisors voted to move the polling place, county officials submitted the change to the U.S. Justice Department for review. Section 5 required that Dinwiddie County show that the change did not worsen the political influence of African Americans in the county.

The Justice Department would have sixty days to review the polling-place change. If the department did not object within that time period, the county could move its polling place to Bott Memorial Church. If the department objected, however, the county would have to continue to use the Cut Bank Hunt Club, unless it convinced a federal court in Washington, DC, that the Bott Memorial Church location would not worsen the influence of African Americans. As an alternative, Dinwiddie County could have bypassed the Justice Department altogether and filed the change with the federal court to decide the issue. In either case, no voting change could be made without higher government approval.

At the end of September, the Justice Department requested more information from county officials. In their investigation, Justice Department analysts discovered that the Cut Bank Hunt

Club, located on the western side of the Darvills Precinct, was a private hunting club with a predominantly black membership. A couple of months before the Dinwiddie County Board of Supervisors voted to move the polling place, the board had received a petition with 105 signatures, asking that the polling place be moved from the Hunt Club three miles southeast to Mansons Church. The petition stated that the polling place should be "more centrally located." The petition also noted that the Mansons Church had agreed to open its doors as a polling place and claimed that it was "well lighted, good parking, [and] handicap accessible [sic]." Only three of the 105 signatories were African American, and only eighteen of them had voted in the previous election. Mansons Church withdrew its offer, however, and in July 1999 Bott Memorial Presbyterian Church offered its building as a polling place. Bott Memorial, located at the extreme eastern end of the precinct, had an almost exclusively white congregation. After reviewing census data and reaching out to voters, Justice Department analysts discovered that the black population was "heavily concentrated" in the western end of the precinct. Justice Department officials found that the Board of Supervisors not only abandoned the desire for a central location but also discounted the recommendation of the county electoral board to keep the polling place at the Hunt Club.

In October 1999, the Justice Department filed an objection and blocked the change. Dinwiddie County did not petition the federal district court.

A POWERFUL TOOL TO FIGHT MANIPULATION BY POLITICIANS

After the Voting Rights Act was passed in 1965, its impact was immediate. In the five years following enactment of the law, as many Southern blacks were registered as had been registered in the previous 100 years. In Mississippi, African-American registration increased from less than 6.7 percent in 1965 to 60 percent in 1968.[2] Some state and local politicians maintained their power by devising election practices that would ensure that white voters would almost always outnumber black voters. Common tactics included redrawing electoral districts, abandoning districts altogether and shifting to countywide elections, and annexing adjacent white communities. In 1969, the U.S. Supreme Court ruled that the Voting Rights Act outlawed such manipulation. The court reasoned that the act protected not only the ability of people of color to cast a vote but also the effectiveness of such a vote.[3]

In the years that followed, the Voting Rights Act was strengthened. The preclearance provision proved so effective that in 1970 Congress extended it for another five years and modified the coverage formula to also include parts of California, Connecticut, Idaho, Maine, Massachusetts, New Hampshire, New York, and Wyoming—all areas that had imposed voting tests and had low voter registration or participation among the electorate as a whole.

In 1975, Congress extended the preclearance provisions another seven years and recognized the need to broaden them to protect Latino, Asian-American, American Indian, and Native Alaskan voters, thus expanding coverage to all of Alaska, Arizona, and Texas, as well as counties in California, Florida, New York, North Carolina, South Dakota, and a few townships in Michigan. These areas had a combination of significant language-minority populations, English-only voting materials, and low turnout. In 1982, Congress renewed the preclearance requirements, this time for twenty-five years.

Congress had reason to be proud of this legislation. Section 5 worked wonders. The number of African-American elected officials in the South jumped from seventy-two in 1965 to almost 2,000 in 1976, and up to almost 5,000 by 1993. The number of Latino federal, state, and local elected officials in Arizona, California, Florida, New Mexico, New York, and Texas increased from 1,280 in 1973 to 3,677 in 1991.[4]

Section 5 continues to be an essential tool in preventing politicians from excluding voters to maintain their own power.

In late 2003, the Waller County (Texas) district attorney, sixty-nine-year-old Republican Oliver Kitzman, sent a letter to county elections administrator Lela Loewe, asserting that students at Prairie View A&M University, a historically black college located in Waller County, were not permanent county residents and thus were ineligible to vote. Kitzman threatened to prosecute the students with a felony if they registered or voted. The letter was published in the *Waller Times* newspaper within a few days.

"Why is this happening again in Waller County?" asked Prairie View A&M Student Body President Henrik Maison. "This was settled twenty-five years ago."

Indeed, previous Waller County officials had attempted similar tactics. From 1966 to 1978, Waller County tax assessor collector Leroy Symm employed a residency questionnaire to effectively disenfranchise most Prairie View students. In 1976, after Symm registered only thirty-five of the 545 potential voters, the Department of Justice filed and eventually won a lawsuit arguing that the forms discriminated against the students.

Oliver Kitzman also had served in county government during the 1970s as district attorney, and he had made headlines back then for his underenforcement of the law. In covering Kitzman's overtures to prosecute Prairie View student voters in 2004, the *Dallas Morning News* reported:

> The last time Oliver Kitzman made big news as a district attorney, the result was a musical comedy, *The Best Little Whorehouse in Texas*, spoofing small-town hypocrisy. . . . In the 1970s, in an

earlier stint as district attorney, [Kitzman] was a peripheral character in the flap over the Chicken Ranch, a house of prostitution in La Grange, 60 miles west of Prairie View. The episode inspired the famous musical. . . . An outraged young reporter named Marvin Zindler . . . accused Mr. Kitzman of turning a blind eye to the shenanigans, the exact opposite of his role as overzealous prosecutor in the Prairie View voting dispute. . . .

Texas's Republican Attorney General Greg Abbott intervened in the 2004 voting controversy, issuing a ruling that no student should be excluded on residency grounds from voting. "Let me be very clear. The right to vote is a fundamental right in this state and in this country," Abbott wrote. "It is the bedrock of democracy and a right that preserves all other basic civil and political rights, and it must be and will be vigorously defended."

But Kitzman persisted in his efforts to eliminate student voters. On February 6, 2004, the Prairie View A&M University chapter of the NAACP, represented by the Lawyers' Committee for Civil Rights, filed a lawsuit to stop his threats to prosecute student voters. The most pressing concern was an upcoming March 9 primary election in which two Prairie View students were running for office, including one for County Board of Commissioners. On February 10, the County Board of Commissioners responded to the lawsuit by voting to reduce early voting in the precinct closest to Prairie View A&M from seventeen hours over two days to six hours in a single day. The reduction in early voting not only would limit the hours that students could vote early but also threatened to affect the election outcome because the students would be on spring break on the day of the actual primary election. On February 17, the Prairie View A&M University NAACP chapter filed a second lawsuit, alleging that the county was seeking to implement a voting change without first obtaining Section 5 preclearance. The board gave in on February 25, agreeing to restore the original hours of early voting at the Prairie View precinct. Kitzman also agreed not to prosecute any student voters.

Section 5 made a significant difference, according to Jon Greenbaum, the director of the Voting Rights Project of the Lawyers' Committee for Civil Rights. "[A]lmost 400 citizens voted at the Prairie View precinct on the second day of early voting, and the Prairie View student running for the Board won his primary by less than 50 votes."[5] Without Section 5, incumbent politicians in Waller County could have simply doctored the election rules, and the outcome most certainly would have been different—and unfair.

RACIAL QUOTAS?

Despite—or perhaps because of—Section 5's effectiveness, it has now come under attack. Affirmative-action critics charge that the law prevents democratic competition and extends a race-based entitlement to unqualified candidates of color at the expense of whites. Ensuring the best leadership, the argument goes, requires that we abolish race-conscious laws like Section 5.

But the preclearance process is not an employment program that entitles candidates of color to a certain quota of legislative seats, or one that gives them extra votes to remedy past discrimination. Instead, Section 5 resembles other laws that prohibit racial discrimination by protecting *voters* from election practices that dilute or diminish their right to vote and to elect candidates. Any benefits to *candidates* are incidental. The racial complexions of elected officials reveal that the law does not guarantee quotas. Americans of color make up approximately 33 percent of citizens and 28.5 percent of registered voters in states covered in whole by Section 5, but they account for less than 13 percent of the local, state, and federal elected officials.

Voters and Elected Officials in Section 5 States[6]

	Registered Voters (%)	*Total Elected Officials (%)*
Asian	1.3	.07
Latino	9.1	3.9
Black	18.1	8.6
White/Anglo	71.3	87.3

Affirmative-action opponents Edward Blum and Roger Clegg also argue that the Voting Rights Act has been a "means of second-guessing perfectly legitimate, nonracial rules" like photo-ID requirements and prohibitions on voting by former felons. But federal law should consider how these local election practices affect people of color. Since the Civil War, politicians have crafted many seemingly "nonracial rules," such as literacy tests and poll taxes, that effectively disenfranchise people of color. Even when such laws are passed without racial animus, they deserve special attention in light of the propensity of self-interested politicians to enact rules that benefit themselves instead of the electorate. Further, the blocking of election rules that disproportionately exclude voters of color often opens democracy to others as well—especially the poor, the less educated, and senior citizens.[7]

AN OUNCE OF PREVENTION

The editorial board of Alabama's largest newspaper, the *Mobile Register*, announced its opposition to Section 5 in March 2005. The editors complained that in today's improved racial climate, the review process is no longer needed, and that the process causes "delays, costs and bureaucratic hassles that themselves make it hard for elected officials to ensure fair and timely elections."

Others have suggested that lawsuits can fix any remaining racial manipulation in politics.[8] But by preventing discriminatory election practices before they are adopted, the relatively inexpensive Section 5 review process is much more efficient than lawsuits.

Since 1965, Section 5 has been used to block more than 1,000 discriminatory voting changes. Although the Justice Department continues to object to about ten voting changes per year, Section 5's most important contribution today is deterrence. When state and local politicians in areas covered by Section 5 debate a voting change, they know that federal officials will eventually review any proposal. As a result, they often consider racial impact and design proposed changes so as not to worsen the position of voters of color. As former Justice Department Attorney Michael Pitts has written:

> Having literally looked at hundreds of redistrictings submitted to the Attorney General, I can attest to the fact that the documents provided by local officials . . . amply demonstrate that local officials and their demographers are acutely cognizant of the standards for preclearance and typically try to steer very clear of anything that would raise concerns with the Attorney General.

Without Section 5, politicians would be even bolder in manipulating the matrix of election practices to enhance their own power. In fact, following the 2003 redistricting in Texas, when Republicans inflated their share of the state's congressional seats from 47 percent to 66 percent, Republican State Representative Phil King, head of the Texas House Redistricting Committee, testified that Republicans aimed to win as many seats as possible, but they were confined by the need to protect minority voting rights.[9] Section 5 put a brake on the politicians' manipulation of district lines.

Even when local officials acting in good faith initially fail to realize that a proposed change has a discriminatory impact, the review process provides valuable feedback and allows them to modify their change voluntarily without going to court or being cited with a legal violation. Before filing an objection to a proposed election change, the Justice Department generally sends out a letter asking for answers to specific questions. The information requested often prompts local officials to realize that the proposed change would harm voters of color. "We hadn't thought of that," local officials commonly explain to Justice Department analysts. At that point, localities often withdraw the submission and avoid receiving an objection from the Justice Department. They later file a revised election practice that achieves the legitimate objectives of their original submission but does not worsen the position of voters of color.

The preclearance process is also less expensive than litigation.

Frances Deberry is the paralegal in the South Carolina attorney general's office who submits the state's election-law changes to the U.S. Justice Department. She estimates that when she first started in 1994, submission preparation took her an average of six months per year to complete. It now requires only four months of her time—three months at the end of the legislative session when bills are produced and another 180 to 200 hours scattered throughout the year. During the remainder of her time, she works with lawyers in the antitrust section of the attorney general's office.

While the numbers vary from year to year, Frances generally submits up to fifty election changes per year. More election changes generally occur in the two-year window following the release of the U.S. Census count, when state and local officials redraw districts for U.S. Congress, the state legislature, and city and county councils and school boards. County election commissions generally submit their own changes to the Justice Department, although they'll often call Frances for her insights. Frances submits revised school-district maps, however, since the state legislature redraws those boundaries.

Preparing a submission can take Frances as little as an hour or as long as a week. "It is almost impossible to estimate the time of each submission because each change is unique," she says. If she suspects that the Justice Department will look more closely at a change from a county school board that has had problems in the recent past, she will spend more time assembling data about that submission.

When she needs demographic data about a change, Frances generally calls Wayne Gilbert in Research & Statistics. Wayne, thirty-nine years old, holds a BA in statistics and an MA in public administration. Since 1992, he has worked as a manager of Geographic Information Systems (GIS) for South Carolina's Office of Research & Statistics. The GIS program is software that's loaded onto a standard desktop computer, allowing one to view and analyze data on a map. For example, by downloading a database of the street-number addresses of homes where burglaries occurred, GIS can print out a map with dots that represent the location of each burglary. Concentrations of dots reveal high crime rates and show police where to focus their enforcement efforts. Wayne uses a couple of GIS software programs—ArcView and AutoBound—to help state and local officials realign district and precinct boundaries. Dots on the maps he produces represent registered voters. If you wanted to move a district boundary two blocks to the west, Wayne could use the GIS program to tell you how many African-American voters you would pick up in the district. Political parties use similar software to tailor election-district maps to their interests.

The amount of time it takes Wayne to respond to a request from Frances varies. If Frances wants a school-board district map and a population summary report that includes race, Wayne works for roughly an hour to pull together the information. He estimates that he spends forty-five hours per year working on projects for her. Once Wayne sends the map and other data back to Frances, she analyzes it. "If I think it's going to be objected to," she says, "I'll

contact a legislator, and tell him, 'Here's what's gone on in the past.'"
If she thinks the change will gain preclearance, she writes a letter
to the Justice Department, explaining the change. She'll also
include the map and any other data she receives from Wayne.

After Frances prepares the package, she sends it to Senior
Assistant Attorney General C. Havird Jones, Jr., also known as
"Sonny." Sonny has twenty-five years' experience reviewing sub-
missions to the Justice Department. It generally takes him roughly
twenty minutes to review the submission and approve it, although
he sometimes spends more time and asks Frances questions. After
Sonny approves the package, Frances sends it to the Justice
Department via registered mail.

Technology also makes compliance much easier for states and
localities than it was in 1982, when Congress extended the preclearance provisions for twenty-five years. Democrat Bob
Sheheen, a former speaker of the South Carolina General
Assembly, guided the reapportionment process to draw the
General Assembly map in the early 1980s. Without the assistance
of GIS software, Sheheen had to take 1,000 pages of new U.S.
Census data and correlate it to a map. It was a cumbersome
process, requiring a team of five people to analyze the new census
data twelve to fourteen hours a day for four weeks to determine
how existing districts were affected. Sheheen estimates that the
group spent about a third of its time over a six-week period analyzing the then-existing black-majority districts to see what
changes had taken place during the time between the 1970 census
and the 1980 census so that the General Assembly would know
what changes to make to comply with one-man, one-vote guidelines and to pass scrutiny under Section 5. The cost to the state in
salaries for the time the team focused on this issue works out to
just above $12,000 (more than $24,000 today, adjusted for inflation). "The amount of time would have been reduced dramatically
with computers," Sheheen says.

Frances Deberry is also more efficient due to technology—and not just from the GIS maps provided by Wayne Gilbert. "It's so much easier," she says. "I've been playing around with computers since 1983. I can't function without them." Frances uses the computer to pull up the existing law that the proposed rule will replace, and she includes the printout in the package to the Justice Department. Rather than going to the library to look up basic information—such as phone numbers of county officials—she can find it on the computer. "I stay on the computer all day long," she raves.

Some costs of the current process are difficult to quantify. Legislative counsel, whom Frances describes as "experienced and knowledgable," consider Section 5 when they draft legislation along with myriad other variables. Also, the U.S. House, General Assembly, and State Senate maps, which are submitted to federal authorities once every ten years, require more resources than the average submission (the state legislature, rather than the attorney general's office, takes charge of the submission process for these three plans). Wayne points out that even in the absence of Section 5, the state would buy GIS software to draw districts (AutoBound software costs less than $4,000 and can process publicly available census data).

Frances, Wayne, and Sonny's hours comprise the vast bulk of costs to the state for most submissions, however. Based on government pay scales, the state annually pays out less than $18,300 in salaries devoted to compliance with Section 5, averaging under $458 per submission in a year with forty submissions.

By comparison, incumbent politicians on the Charleston County Council spent more than $1.5 million of taxpayer funds fighting a single voting-rights lawsuit against the Justice Department. The costs of attorneys, expert witnesses, depositions, travel, and responding to requests for documents added up quickly. Courts consistently held that the county council's districting system—which benefited the incumbent politicians—violated the Voting

Rights Act. After various appeals, the matter was finally resolved in 2005, four years after it was filed (the county council lost). A single voting-rights lawsuit can also require extensive spending by both the Justice Department (more than $1 million if the case goes to trial) and the court system.

By preventing problems before they occur, the preclearance process provides many of the same benefits over litigation as the federal Hart-Scott-Rodino review process. (That federal antitrust procedure protects American consumers by requiring that companies submit information about proposed mergers worth more than $56.7 million to the federal government for review. Unlike Section 5 preclearance, however, Hart-Scott-Rodino requires a filing fee of at least $45,000.)

Despite the efficiency of Section 5, litigation is still needed in certain situations. Whereas Section 5 only blocks new discriminatory voting proposals, lawsuits allow plaintiffs to challenge any election procedure that is unfair to voters of color (even one that's been on the books for a century). While the Section 5 review process is administered by the government, litigation provides a forum for average citizens to protect their voting rights. The targeted Section 5 review process serves as an important complement to litigation, deterring and blocking discriminatory election changes, preventing unnecessary lawsuits, and ensuring that limited litigation and judicial resources are used most efficiently.

Former legislator Bob Sheheen's 1981 General Assembly map was South Carolina's first state legislative map that made it through Justice Department review without an objection. With regard to complying with Section 5, Sheheen didn't whine. "I got elected to follow the law, I recognized that this is the law of the land, and I tried to pass [district maps] in accordance with the law," Sheheen says. The former speaker also prefers to avoid being the target of litigation. "I like to think that I am a good lawyer, a lousy witness, but a particularly bad defendant when named in a lawsuit."

"Reviewing these changes saves our state money in the long run by avoiding potential lawsuits," says Wayne Gilbert, who is African American. "I can't speak about other places, but in a state like South Carolina, we need this kind of process."[10]

ABUSING THE VOTING RIGHTS ACT FOR PARTISAN GAIN?

Samuel Issacharoff is a professor of law at New York University. As a young attorney in the 1980s, Issacharoff litigated voting-rights cases for the Lawyers' Committee for Civil Rights in Washington, DC. While his courtroom presence made him popular among students when he started teaching in the early 1990s, Issacharoff established himself among scholars by churning out three or four important articles every year and coauthoring a leading voting-rights textbook. Much of his writing focused on the tendency of politicians to design election rules that diminish competition by benefiting themselves or their parties.

In a provocative article entitled "Is Section 5 of the Voting Rights Act a Victim of Its Own Success?" Issacharoff suggests that the Section 5 process does more harm than good because it invites partisan enforcement by the Justice Department. He notes that when the Voting Rights Act was passed in 1965, the South was entirely Democratic. As a result, denying preclearance in Southern states benefited voters of color, instead of one party at the expense of the other. Today, however, since most whites in the South have abandoned the Democratic Party for the Republican Party, and most blacks remain Democrats, the political appointees in the Justice Department can abuse their preclearance power to benefit their political allies on the local level. A Republican Justice Department, for example, might construe a redistricting plan that favors Democrats as harming voters of color. A Democratic Justice

Department can do the same to reject Republican-sponsored redistricting.

Mike Pitts, age thirty-four, disagrees with Issacharoff. After college, Pitts worked at the Justice Department as a preclearance analyst reviewing election changes submitted by states and localities. Upon graduating from Georgetown Law School, Pitts returned to the Justice Department as a lawyer working on Section 5 matters. He has written about the Voting Rights Act, and one of his articles—"Let's Not Call the Whole Thing Off Just Yet"—responds to Issacharoff.

Pitts acknowledges that the partisanship problem exists, but he points out that Issacharoff overlooks checks within the Voting Rights Act that diminish partisan manipulation. For example, if a Democratic Virginia state legislature fears that its redistricting map will be rejected by a partisan Republican Justice Department, it can bypass the department and request that a three-judge federal court in Washington preclear the plan. These judges, appointed by presidents for life, are generally less susceptible to partisan pressure.[11]

Further, Issacharoff focuses on manipulation of district boundaries, but he overlooks the fact that only 2.25 percent of the election changes submitted under Section 5 to the Justice Department between 1982 and 2004 involved redistricting. While allegations of partisan manipulation in reviewing redistricting should not be ignored (61 percent of Justice Department objections between 1997 and 2002 involved redistricting), our fixation on redistricting should not overshadow Section 5's important role in deterring manipulation of nondistricting election rules.

The fact is, political appointees in the "front office" at the Justice Department are likely to have a political interest in only a very small class of submissions—primarily redistricting for U.S. House seats, because these maps determine which party controls Congress. To a lesser extent, Justice Department appointees may have a passing interest in other statewide changes, such as State House and State Senate maps that determine which party controls state legislatures.

But Justice Department officials generally have minimal political interest in other changes, such as annexations, the calling of special elections, precinct realignments, city/county government consolidations, redistricting of local commissions and school boards (many of which are nonpartisan), and changes to polling-place locations and candidate-qualification requirements.

And Section 5 plays its most significant role by protecting voters on the local level. More than 90 percent of the election-change submissions are from cities, towns, counties, school districts, and other local political bodies; between 2000 and 2004, 92 percent of the Justice Department's objections were directed at these levels of government. Also, without Section 5, local election abuses are most likely to go undetected and unremedied. Partisan abuse in drawing state legislative or congressional districts attracts statewide and sometimes national media attention, and political players and civil-rights organizations often file lawsuits. But when thousands of small counties, cities, and towns across the country change their voting procedures, abuses are more difficult to detect. Major media outlets and civil-rights organizations with expertise in analyzing voting data are less likely to scrutinize these local changes. Even voters of color on the local level who suspect an election change is harmful are often less able—sometimes because of the change itself—to express their dissatisfaction through the political process.

Issacharoff also suggests that Section 5 is no longer needed because today people of color can work within the political system to ensure that they receive fair treatment. But we can't always rely on politicians to prevent racial exclusion. Take, for example, the Democratic Party, which is supported by a majority of Asian-American, American Indian, and Latino voters, and an overwhelming majority of African Americans. Moderate Democrats often avoid discussions of race and voting rights, afraid that they will be perceived as the "black" or "brown" party and lose swing voters, especially in the South. Also, Democrats' primary interest is winning elections, not the protection of voting rights. Thus, party operatives have incentives to spread out reliably Democratic voters of color to ensure that Democrats win as many congressional and state legislative seats as possible—even if that means that the perspectives of people of color are diluted in the political process. Republicans, on the other hand, might want to herd all of the voters of color into as few districts as possible to ensure that the maximum number of remaining districts lean Republican. Most politicians focus, first and foremost, on immediate political gain. To the extent we allow political gladiators to define voting rights, the rules of voting will largely advantage incumbent politicians or party interests rather than individual voters. We see this phenomenon not only among voters of color but also among all American voters—as discussed in detail in the first chapter's exploration of partisan, self-serving redistricting and election administration practices. We cannot rely on politicians alone to protect our voting rights.

For that reason, we should preserve the Section 5 review process—one of the few checks that focuses on the interests of voters rather than of politicians—for the vast majority of submissions. In most situations, Justice Department officials have no vested interest and have earned a better track record protecting voting rights than have state and local political operatives. But because Justice Department officials may be vested in the political impact of statewide redistricting maps for U.S. House and state legislative seats and other statewide election practices, we should remove Justice Department authority over these submissions and require that they be reviewed only by a panel of federal judges in Washington, DC.

DISCRIMINATING AGAINST THE SOUTH?

In the first of his dissents rebuking Section 5, United States Supreme Court Justice Hugo Black wrote in 1966 that states should be able to pass election laws without first having to "beg federal authorities to approve them." The preclearance provisions, Justice Black argued, "create the impression that the State or States treated in this way are little more than conquered provinces."[12]

But covered states are "conquered provinces" only insofar as they do not enjoy unbridled freedom to adopt election practices that exclude voters. Chapter 2 examined the various provisions in the Constitution that address federal oversight of state elections. The Fifteenth Amendment, for example, prohibits discrimination in voting and explicitly states: "The Congress shall have power to enforce this article by appropriate legislation." In upholding the preclearance provisions in 1999, the U.S. Supreme Court wrote that "the Reconstruction Amendments by their nature contemplate some intrusion into areas traditionally reserved to the States."[13] And the federal government has generally exercised its constitutional authority with restraint—the Justice Department has objected to only about one percent of the changes submitted under Section 5.

While Justice Black and others inflate the Voting Rights Act's intrusion on "states' rights," an important question persists. Why does federal law treat states differently? Why should the preclearance requirements apply to Virginia, for example, while Maryland is exempt? In March 2005, the editorial page of Alabama's *Mobile Register* commented:

In today's United States, 140 years after the Civil War and 40 years after passage of the original Voting Rights Act of 1965, there is no reason to treat Southern states differently than other states. Indeed, in the last 30 years, some of the most violent racial dust-ups have occurred in other parts of the country, such as Boston in the 1970s. . . .

The problem with the current system is that it treats the Southern states as guilty until proven innocent, and makes all those states' residents into second-class citizens compared to the rest of the country.

The newspaper was right. The South is disproportionately covered by Section 5. Eight of the eleven former states of the Confederacy are covered by Section 5 in whole, and significant parts of North Carolina are also covered (only Arkansas and Tennessee need not preclear their election changes). Section 5 touches on only 18 percent of states outside of the former Confederacy, including all of Alaska and Arizona and parts of California, Michigan, New Hampshire, New York, and South Dakota.[14]

History suggests, however, that we should proceed cautiously in relaxing civil-rights protections. After bartering to end Reconstruction only eleven years after the Civil War, the South reestablished election practices that drove African-American voters from the political process for more than eight decades. Granted, more than forty years have passed since Congress enacted the Voting Rights Act. But the post-Reconstruction period shows that, without effective federal protection of voting rights, the costs of backsliding are high.[15]

Further, under current law, any area, including Southern states and localities, can be removed from the preclearance requirements if it has complied with the law for ten years, has no literacy tests or similar devices, and has no voting-discrimination lawsuit pending against it. Most recently, six counties and three cities in Virginia have "bailed out" and no longer have to preclear their election changes. Before that, five states that were partially covered—Connecticut, Idaho, Maine, Massachusetts, and Wyoming—successfully bailed out under an earlier version of the law. Gerry Hebert is a voting-rights lawyer in Washington, DC, who helped the Virginia counties and cities secure their bailouts. Based on his meetings with state and local officials over the years, more states and localities have not bailed out because many are unaware of the bailout option. State and local officials who know about the procedure often erroneously believe that the bailout process is expensive. Other state and local officials assume that the stamp of Justice Department preclearance approval makes a new election rule easier to defend if it is challenged in court under other voting-rights laws.[16]

But despite the availability of a bailout, there's still the question of whether a 1960s coverage formula most accurately targets voting problems in the twenty-first century. Section 5 preclearance requirements apply to areas that in 1964, 1968, or 1972 required voters to pass a literacy test or similar device and had voter-registration or turnout rates of less than 50 percent. Section 5 also applies to areas that in 1972 provided election materials only in English, while having a language-minority group that accounted for more than 5 percent of voting-age citizens and voter registration or participation rates of less than 50 percent.[17] The attitudes toward race in the South and other covered areas have changed since the early 1970s. Further, the influx and exodus of residents in the past forty years has shifted our nation's population—including people of color. (Between 1995 and 2000 alone, five million people migrated into the South and 3.2 million left.)[18]

Recognizing the changes in the South and the effectiveness of Section 5 in fighting voting discrimination, one might ask, Why not just expand the law so that it is permanent and applies nationwide? While such a move might increase annual enforcement and compliance costs fourfold, one could easily argue that this cost would be well worth the enhanced voting-rights protections.

Some argue, however, that nationwide application would make Section 5 susceptible to constitutional attack. The U.S. Supreme Court has held that federal laws must be "congruent and proportional" to the harms they are intended to address, in order to avoid states'-rights concerns. Also, laws that categorize by race must be "narrowly tailored." While these concerns are likely overblown, targeted application of Section 5 is less vulnerable to challenges in court.

There are other practical concerns. In the past, Section 5 skeptics proposed nationwide application as a means to sink the entire law, speculating that congressional representatives might oppose the law if their home states were covered. Expanding the law might also hamper Justice Department efforts to concentrate resources effectively on the most problematic areas.

Assuming nationwide application is off the table, then the question is whether the states covered by Section 5 continue to pose the greatest threat to voters of color and whether they should remain subject to its requirements. The old literacy and interpretation tests no longer exist, but have new devices taken their place? Some have characterized felon-disenfranchisement rules and photo-ID requirements as modern-day voting tests. As of 2005, three of the four states that barred voting by all ex-felons who had completed their sentences—Alabama, Florida, and Virginia—were covered in whole or in part by the preclearance provisions. Over 56 percent of the states covered by Section 5 requested documentary identification at the polls in 2005, compared with only 38 percent of the uncovered states. (Seventy-two percent of all Southern states had ID requirements, compared with only 36 percent of all states outside of the South.) As explored in chapters 2 and 6, former-felon voting prohibitions and photo-ID rules serve as hurdles to a significant percentage of voters of color. [19]

Socioeconomic factors like racial disparities in income and education might also be relevant to preclearance coverage. People who are poorer and less educated are less likely to vote and be engaged in the political process. Those who do vote are more likely to fail to comply with the regulatory minutiae of voting, such as perfectly perforating a punch-card ballot, standing in two-hour lines, or flaw-lessly filling out a detailed voter registration form. Some politicians may oppose spending more on elections because they believe poor and less-educated voters of color will likely cast ballots for their opponents. Those with less education and income are often less able to organize, make large political contributions, or use other tools to engage in the political process. Educational and income disparities along racial lines may also reflect a political process's failure to respond to the needs of particular communities. The fif-teen states with the largest gap between the median household income of whites and the largest racial minority group in the state include: *Louisiana*, Wisconsin, Rhode Island, *Mississippi*, Minnesota, *Texas*, Connecticut, *California*, *South Carolina*, *Alaska*, Iowa, Massachusetts, Arkansas, Illinois, and Colorado. The fifteen states with the largest gap in those who hold a bachelor's degree between whites and the largest racial minority group in the state are: *California*, *Alaska*, *Arizona*, Colorado, Idaho, *Texas*, Nevada, Wyoming, Nebraska, Utah, New Mexico, *South Dakota*, *South Carolina*, Montana, and Connecticut. (Italics indicate that a state is currently covered by Section 5, either all or in part.)

Felon disenfranchisement, ID rules, and socioeconomic factors do not exclude voters of color to the same degree as literacy and character tests did in the Jim Crow South. Further, some would assert that felon disenfranchisement and voter ID requirements are justified, and others might claim that the nexus between socioeconomic factors and the political process is insufficient to warrant preclearance coverage. In the absence of literacy and interpretation tests, the number of recent voting rights objections and claims by the Justice Department, as well as the number of federal observers sent to monitor elections, are good predictors for where problems are most likely to arise in the immediate future.

The original test also restricted coverage to areas that suffered from voter registration or participation of less than 50 percent. In the 2000 and 2004 presidential elections, only a few states had voter participation of less than 50 percent of voting-age residents. These included four states currently covered by the preclearance provisions (Arizona, California, Georgia, and Texas) and two uncovered states (Hawaii and Nevada). Why should Arizona be subject to Section 5 and not Hawaii?

While the appeal of the original formula was its simplicity, its shortcoming was its failure to fully capture the underlying problems. For example, the original test examined low voter participation among all voters and could miss an area that had very high participation among whites but excluded people of color. Further, the problems are different today. Today's politicians don't exclude all voters of color but instead use sophisticated measures such as annexations and redistricting to dilute the voting strength of communities of color, and hurdles such as polling-place changes to shave off votes from targeted communities. In measuring where preclearance coverage is most needed today, we should consider a more comprehensive and penetrating array of factors that focus on the core problems. The *Mobile Register* is right to suggest that we should not design policy based on outdated stereotypes about the South. But facts must be more recent, quantifiable, and related to actual voting patterns rather than the "violent racial dust-ups" in "Boston in the 1970s" that the *Register* used to assert that Alabama was no different than the uncovered state of Massachusetts.

Structural hurdles to political participation and the engagement of voters of color in politics seem relevant in measuring the health of a state's political process. With these variables in mind, I have compiled a list of eight factors to identify the states that are most susceptible to political practices that disadvantage voters of color. Again, states in italics are covered currently in whole or in part by Section 5. For a detailed explanation of the ranking system's criteria, see the Appendix.

INDICATORS OF POLITICAL EXCLUSION°

1. **Most Voting Rights Act objections and claims per capita:** *South Carolina, Louisiana, Mississippi,* Montana, North Dakota, *South Dakota, Georgia, Virginia,* New Mexico, *Texas, North Carolina, Alabama, Arizona,* New Jersey, and Massachusetts.

2. **Most federal observers sent to monitor elections per capita:** *Mississippi,* New Mexico, *Arizona,* New Jersey, Utah, *Alabama, Michigan,* Washington, Indiana, *California, Louisiana, South Carolina, New York,* Pennsylvania, and Illinois.

3. **Largest disparities between citizens of color and statewide elected officials of color:** *Mississippi,* Maryland, *Louisiana, New York, California, South Carolina, Texas, Florida, Alabama, Virginia, Georgia, North Carolina,* Delaware, *Arizona,* and Arkansas.

4. **Largest disparities between citizens of color and officials of color in all elected positions:** *Texas, New York, California,* Maryland, New Jersey, *Florida, Mississippi,* Delaware, *Georgia,* Nevada, *Virginia, Louisiana,* Illinois, *South Carolina,* and Connecticut.

5. **Least party competition for voters of color:** *Mississippi, Louisiana,* Maryland, Illinois, *Georgia, Tennessee, Alabama, New York,* Arkansas, *Florida, Michigan,* Pennsylvania, *South Carolina, North Carolina,* and Delaware.

6. **Largest racial disparities in voter turnout:** Nevada, California, *Arizona,* Colorado, *Texas,* Connecticut, Massachusetts, New Mexico, *Florida, New York,* Delaware, Oklahoma, *Virginia,* New Jersey, and Indiana.

7. **Largest minority group:** Hawaii, New Mexico, *Mississippi, Louisiana, South Carolina, Georgia,* Maryland, *Alabama,*

°*Section 5 currently applies to all or parts of the states listed in italics.*

California, North Carolina, Virginia, Delaware, Arizona, and
Arkansas.

8. **Largest low-English-proficient populations:** New Mexico,
   Arizona, Hawaii, Alaska, Texas, Connecticut, California, New
   Jersey, Massachusetts, Rhode Island, Colorado, Florida, Nevada,
   New York, and Idaho.[20]

While the lists help us identify places that should remain covered, there are other important variables. The lists fail to consider
intangibles that evade objective measurement. For example, within
the past ten years, politicians in Mississippi, Georgia, and South
Carolina have used Confederate-flag debates to polarize voters
along racial lines. Politicians in California, Texas, and other states
have shown their willingness to manipulate district lines to protect
incumbents or give an advantage to one party. But quantifying such
variables as the Confederate flag or the willingness of politicians to
manipulate election rules is difficult, at least in ranking states.
Similarly, voters' tendency to cast ballots along racial lines is a relevant factor, but we don't have a comprehensive database on
racially polarized voting in every political contest in the nation that
allows a comparative analysis among states (although the dearth of
statewide elected officials of color and the lack of party competition
for voters of color are rough proxies for racially polarized voting).
Startling reports about recent voting discrimination against
American Indians in South Dakota have also emerged, so perhaps
parts of that state should remain covered.

We should also limit preclearance coverage to areas that have a
significant percentage of people of color. In such areas, discrimination may be more rampant because voters of color likely carry more
political weight. If we were to exclude states that lack a single
minority group that makes up at least 5 percent of the population,
we would release New Hampshire from current coverage. We also

would not consider expanding coverage to Iowa, Maine, Minnesota, North Dakota, Vermont, or West Virginia.[21] A better approach would apply the 5 percent test to counties within these states, thereby allowing coverage for a single county with heavier concentrations of voters of color.

Checks and balances have been a part of our nation since its inception, and they are especially important in protecting democracy today. Section 5 of the Voting Rights Act is one of the most effective checks to ensure that self-interested state and local politicians do not manipulate election rules in a way that excludes American voters.

Another critical provision of the Voting Rights Act requires certain counties and states to provide bilingual ballots and other language assistance to make politicians more responsive to all of the people. But as the next chapter will show, the voting rights of millions of Americans are currently under siege by a network of groups who believe that democracy should be withheld from Americans with limited English skills.

CHAPTER FIVE

LA SOCIEDAD ABIERTA*

In August 1984, two nights of riots hit Lawrence, Massachusetts—a city of 72,000 people located thirty miles north of Boston. Buildings were firebombed. More than two dozen people were injured and about the same number were arrested. City officials declared a state of emergency and imposed a three-day curfew.

While politicians characterized the riots as a family feud, Latino residents told the *New York Times* that local whites hurled a stone through the window of a Latino family's home and ignited pent-up racial tensions. "The police officers treat us like animals," said Angel Schmidt, a Latino in his mid-twenties. Isabel Melendez, who worked for the Greater Lawrence Community Action Council, told the *Times*: "There are a lot of frustrations: lack of housing, people unprepared to join the job market, poverty."

A group of white youths said that the conflict was "strictly racial," and that they "hoped there would be more trouble." One businessman in his sixties, who refused to be identified, said of the violence: "It had to come. This used to be a good city but you get all these

La Sociedad Abierta means "Open Society."

Spanish people in here and 90 percent of them don't work." Referring to the crowds of Latinos outside a local welfare office, he claimed, "You never see a white person there."

In the 1920s, immigrants of French-Canadian and Irish descent worked in Lawrence's textile mills. The Great Depression prompted an exodus of textile manufacturers to the South in search of cheap labor, and the town's economy never recovered. In the 1960s, Latinos started to settle in Lawrence, steadily increasing to an estimated 20 percent of the town's population by 1984. Most were Puerto Rican or Dominican.

Isabel Melendez was among the first. She was born in Puerto Rico, and in 1959, at the age of twenty-two, she moved to Lawrence with her husband. "It was very easy to come here—jobs and housing were easy to get," explained Isabel. "Even people who didn't speak the language were welcomed to fill the jobs in the shoe factories."

In 1986—two years after the riots—Kevin Sullivan, a twenty-six-year-old Democratic alderman of Irish ancestry, was elected mayor of Lawrence. Isabel supported Sullivan's opponent, who she believed would be more responsive to the needs and concerns of the Latino community. By contrast, she felt that Sullivan's message amounted to, "Let's give the city back to those who built it."

Sullivan identified Lawrence's primary problems as drugs, welfare fraud, and illegal immigration. By targeting enforcement efforts at welfare recipients suspected of drug-related crimes and confiscating welfare cards during drug raids, Sullivan reduced drug trafficking, cut welfare rolls, and ejected illegal immigrants. But two-thirds of Lawrence's 13,000 welfare recipients were Latino, and Sullivan's efforts drew claims of discrimination. The mayor's "attacks on Hispanics and the poor are at best unsupported demagoguery," Lawrence Human Rights Commissioner Guilmo Barrio wrote in a letter to the *Lawrence Eagle-Tribune* just before resigning from his post in protest. "At worst, they are vicious half truths designed to inflame racial and class hatred."

State officials were also skeptical of Sullivan's tactics. "We're all totally opposed to drug abuse and welfare fraud," state Welfare Commissioner Carmen Canino-Siegrist told the *Boston Globe*. "But what they do when they seize those cards is take away an opportunity for a mother to put food on the table." The state Department of Public Welfare estimated that only 15 percent of seized welfare cards in Lawrence stemmed from drug arrests, and the remainder arose from crimes such as disorderly conduct, shoplifting, and loitering. Sullivan disputed those figures and accused state officials of tolerating widespread welfare fraud.

In response to the raids, a federal court banned Lawrence police from confiscating food-stamp and Medicaid cards during drug raids. Sullivan criticized "liberal judges who just don't get it," and explained: "[W]e have people coming here from all over the world because of the social service system we have in place now." In 1991, the mayor left the Democratic Party and became a Republican.

Education was also an issue. By 1990, approximately 70 percent of the students in Lawrence Public Schools were Latino, but no one on the seven-member school committee was Latino. State officials estimated that more than half of Lawrence's 212 bilingual education classes violated state pupil-teacher–ratio regulations. Mayor Sullivan and Lawrence School Superintendent James F. Scully asserted that the troubles were related to finances, not race. "Something has to give," Superintendent Scully told the *Boston Globe*. "Let me say I put bilingual education in compliance, then what do I do? Do I drive regular education up to 35 or 40 per class?"

Unlike most Massachusetts school systems, Lawrence spent more per pupil on regular students than on bilingual students. Figures showed that Lawrence spent $3,981 per student in regular classes and only $2,986 per student in its bilingual program, compared with a statewide average of $3,894 per regular education student and $4,278 for each bilingual student. Isabel Melendez noted that most of the city's Latino students went to school on the city's north side, while most of the white children attended better schools on the city's south side. With schools—and other city services—"it was like two cities," she said.

"The priority of the current administration is not education, but public safety and not public safety for Latinos or people in the housing projects but the white minority still hanging on in the city—mainly the elderly because they tend to vote," Jorge Santiago, executive director of a human-services agency, explained to the *Boston Globe*. Although Latinos had increased to 25 percent of Lawrence's voting-age-citizen population by 1990, they comprised only 11 percent of registered voters. Even those Latinos registered were less likely than Anglos to vote.

Various explanations were given for the voting disparities. Mayor Sullivan told the *Boston Globe* that thousands of Latinos were more interested in politics in the Dominican Republic than in Lawrence. Carlos Matos, an organizer of the Latino Voting Rights Committee of Lawrence, told the local newspaper that many Latinos were too "turned off" to participate in Lawrence politics. "I think the issue of being a stakeholder is paramount to the process of voter participation, the matter of whether people participate in elections or even bother getting registered," said Matos. "For many years, I think Latinos have been ignored and not felt a part of the process. We've seen this with the School Committee, where parents' opinions have been ignored."

Carol Hardy Fanta, a researcher with the Mauricio Gastón Institute for Latino Community Development and Public Policy at the University of Massachusetts, suggested to the *Boston Globe* that the blame rested with the political status quo: "In the old days the political parties really reached out to immigrants. Now I think the prevailing sentiment is 'don't rock the boat' with newcomers that can't be controlled."

And then there were the demographic factors. More than a third of Latino residents hailed from the Dominican Republic, and many were ineligible to vote because they had not been in the United States long enough to become citizens. The Latino population was also younger. Only 62 percent of Lawrence's Latinos were old enough to vote, compared with 78 percent of the Anglos.

In addition to citizenship and age, some claimed that the voting process itself discouraged Latino voters and candidates. Latinos told the *Boston Globe* that election workers demanded identification at the polls, refused to assist them with voting instructions, and made the process difficult and alienating. "As a result, people get frustrated and don't go to vote," said Dalia Diaz, editor of *Rumbo*, a Spanish-language newspaper in Lawrence. "I kept my eyes and ears open when I went to vote. There were no postings about voter assistance, there was nothing in Spanish. Hispanics are not made to feel welcome."

Isabel was one of the first Latinos to volunteer at the polls, where she noticed that English-only ballots were a problem for many Latinos who had limited English skills. She remembers one citizen who brought a friend to the polling place to help him read the ballot, only to be told—erroneously—that he could not have bilingual assistance. Moreover, the "polling workers didn't always understand questions" from Spanish speakers, leading to further frustrations for Latino voters. During this period, Isabel often encountered angry reactions from whites. "Many times, I was told, 'My parents came here and they learned English, so can everyone else.' But I would respond, 'Just because a person can't speak the language doesn't mean they can't vote.'"

Lawrence fell under the Voting Rights Act's language-assistance requirements. While the original Voting Rights Act in 1965 focused on protecting African-American voters in the South, Congress added the language-assistance provisions in 1975 in response to claims of political exclusion of language minorities—particularly Latinos in Texas. The provisions require that Lawrence (and other areas with significant numbers of language minorities) provide language assistance at every step of the process, such as bilingual registration forms and ballots, bilingual registration clerks and poll workers to give oral assistance, and publicity that bilingual assistance is available.

Isabel indicated that she and others in the community took their concerns to the city, but they were told that the city had more pressing needs and could not afford to implement language-assistance provisions. "The response was not what we were looking for," she remembered. Several members of the group took their concerns to the Department of Justice, and soon federal lawyers were interviewing Isabel and other Latino residents.

In 1998, the U.S. Department of Justice sued the City of Lawrence for violating the Voting Rights Act. Justice Department attorneys determined that Latino political influence was diminished by the city's failure to provide bilingual election materials, bloc voting by white voters against candidates preferred by Latinos, and citywide rather than district elections for most positions. Although Latinos were a majority of city residents, Ralph L. Carrero was the sole Latino on the seven-member school committee and Jose Santiago was the only Latino on the nine-member city council. "Hispanic citizens in Lawrence have faced significant and numerous barriers in casting an effective vote," said Acting U.S. Assistant Attorney General for Civil Rights, Bill Lann Lee. "Our lawsuit is a comprehensive enforcement effort designed to eliminate those barriers."

Local officials in Lawrence fumed over the lawsuit, including Democrat Patricia Dowling, the Anglo mayor who succeeded Kevin Sullivan in 1998 (Dowling would later tap Sullivan's brother, Michael, to replace her as mayor). "The real crux of the complaint appears to be that the Justice Department would like to see more

Hispanics elected in Lawrence," Mayor Dowling told the *Boston Globe*. "They want to change the way people are elected in this city. But this is a local issue." Dowling also asserted that the Justice Department appeared focused only on race: "I find that divisive. Aren't people elected based on qualifications?"

Tom Duggan, who runs a Web site that features local issues, was less measured:

> For years Lawrence has seen many immigrant groups flock to what we half heartedly call the immigrant city. Italian, German, French and yes even Irish immigrants were once the new kids on the block. . . . Only after overcoming poverty, cultural, and language differences did those minorities gradually became policemen, business owners, city councilors and yes, even Mayors, and State Representatives. But it didn't happen over night [*sic*]. And it certainly did not happen by the federal government bullying local officials into changing the city charter for people who had not yet paid their dues. . . . What is most disturbing to me is that now, the federal government is stepping in to force our City Charter to accommodate, perhaps even cater to minorities in city elections. . . . I always thought that lumping people together based on ethnicity was racism and that the government was suppose [*sic*] to fight such racism? . . . The Fed should worry more about drugs and illegal aliens coming onto [*sic*] the country than forcing their liberal philosophies on poor communities that can't defend themselves.

In 1999, Lawrence city officials settled part of the lawsuit and agreed to provide bilingual voting information, ballots, and poll workers. The city also committed to disseminating election information through local Spanish-language media and community groups.

By 2001, the voting-rights lawsuit, combined with grassroots registration drives and the more convenient voter-registration requirements of the 1993 National Voter Registration Act ("Motor Voter
Act"), helped increase Latino registration. Latinos, who by now
comprised more than 60 percent of Lawrence residents, made up
43.7 percent of the city's registered voters. The nonpartisan 2001
mayoral race featured former Mayor Kevin Sullivan's brother,
forty-four-year old Republican City Councilman Michael Sullivan,
against Democrat Isabel Melendez, who was by now a sixty-three-
year-old radio host.

When Isabel first prevailed in a six-person primary that allowed
her to face Sullivan, she decided, "I wanted a clean campaign, and
no personal attacks." Sullivan also set and met high standards for
his campaign, and the race was "very professional." Isabel said people still talk about it as a benchmark for a civil political campaign.
In the end, Sullivan reached out to Latinos, spent three times as
much as Melendez, and won by 957 votes. Despite the outcome,
Isabel revealed, "I didn't feel like a loser. I felt like a winner
because we were going to work out the issues facing the community." She remembered that Sullivan talked to her after the election, saying, "I'm going to be listening."

A few months later, Mayor Michael Sullivan's administration settled the remaining claims of the voting-rights lawsuit by agreeing
that six of the school-committee members would be elected from
districts rather than citywide, and the mayor would serve as chair.
The city would also appoint a bilingual member to its Board of
Registrars of Voters and a full-time bilingual staff member to the
City Hall elections office.

By 2005, Latino students accounted for 90 percent of the
Lawrence school-system enrollment. Latinos held two of the seven
school-committee seats and four of the nine city-council seats.
Michael Sullivan remained mayor. On its Web site, the city
described itself as follows:

Known as the "Immigrant City," Lawrence has always been a multi-ethnic and multicultural gateway city with a high proportion of foreign-born residents. The successive waves of immigrants coming to Lawrence to work in the mills began with the Irish, followed by French Canadians, Englishmen, and Germans in the late 1800s. Around the turn of the century and early 1900s, Italians, Poles, Lithuanians, and Syrians began arriving. The wave of Puerto Ricans and Dominicans started in the mid–late 1900s, and the newest arrivals originate from Vietnam and Cambodia. The current population of roughly 70,000 is largely Hispanic and has given a Latino slant to the local economy and culture.

Does Lawrence now provide more for all of its residents? That's a question best left to its citizens to answer. Isabel indicated that as mayor, Michael Sullivan has followed through on his promise to her, and "He has been very close to the community." She attributes much of the responsiveness of the city's politicians to bilingual ballots and increased Latino political participation. "People no longer are afraid to vote," she said. "We make sure that we have bilingual staff in each and every polling place. I'm always watching that, and right now I'm training people to work in the polls." As a result, she believes, "there's much more interaction" between politicians and whites and the city's Latino residents. "It's reality. Latinos are getting involved. The numbers are increasing every day," she claimed. "They have to work for the Latino vote now. Sooner or later, we're going to have a Latino mayor. We're going to have more Latinos in elected positions."

Greater Latino participation has forced candidates and elected officials of all backgrounds to consider diverse perspectives in running for office and making decisions.[1] But even beyond politics, Isabel believes that bilingual ballots and increased Latino political participation have affected the race relations and quality of life in her city. "We have had no major problems since 1994," she explained, beaming with pride. "Lawrence is unique. There's no other city in Massachusetts like it."

And she has noticed the trend much closer to home. "I was shocked when my twenty-four-year-old grandson, James, said he was going to run for City Council. He's watching the news and reading about politics." She sees the results in Latino children, too. "You listen to the kids, and they're talking about politics now," Isabel observed. "This week, I saw two young people talking, and I heard one say, 'One day, I'm going to be mayor.' "[2]

Although bilingual ballots open democracy to Americans in Lawrence and other towns across the nation, some argue that translations at the polls are unnecessary and expensive and breed divisiveness. Congress enacted the Voting Rights Act's language-assistance requirements in 1975 for seven years; in 1982, it extended the provisions for ten years, and in 1992 for fifteen years. In the period leading up to the sunset of the language-assistance provisions in 2007, several groups and politicians campaigned against renewing the provisions. Republican U.S. Congressman Peter King of New York represents parts of two counties required to provide bilingual ballots in Spanish, but King has twice introduced legislation that would repeal the Voting Rights Act's language-assistance provisions. Although his bill has yet to make it out of committee, fifty-one members of Congress cosponsored King's most recent proposal.

The bilingual-ballot debate raises larger questions: With a diverse citizenry featuring multiple languages, racial groups, cultures, physical abilities, and economic classes, how do we balance government's obligation to make voting accessible against an individual's responsibility for casting his or her own vote? To what extent should election officials invest resources to maximize voter participation through bilingual ballots, better and more accessible voting machines and polling locations, and other practices that make voting easier?[3]

BILINGUAL BALLOTS: BRIDGE OR BARRIER?

The arguments against language assistance at the polls resemble those used to oppose bilingual education and other multilingual policies. Groups such as English First, ProEnglish, and U.S. English claim that the English language unites our nation of immigrants while multiple languages divide our country along ethnic lines. Widespread translations are paternalistic, obstruct assimilation, and cheat recent immigrants out of opportunities enjoyed by those who came from such countries as Germany and Italy in earlier generations—or so the argument goes. Language is not an immutable characteristic like skin color—everyone in the United States should be expected to learn English as quickly as possible. Further, multilingual policies are usually more costly and ineffective than a policy that conducts all societal business in English, as realized by the majority of states that have adopted English as their official state language. In the words of Dr. Samuel Ichiye Hayakawa, whom U.S. English proudly proclaims as its founder, "Bilingualism for the individual is fine, but not for a country."

While these points may seem hostile to some, they make sense to many Americans, including "Six Million Dollar Man" Lee Majors, golfer Arnold Palmer, and California Governor Arnold Schwarzenegger (all sit on U.S. English's advisory board). They also resonate with many Americans who have struggled to understand a cashier at their local McDonald's or 7-Eleven. At the other end of the spectrum, multiculturalists argue that hostility toward other languages reflects the insecurity of provincial English speakers who hope to maintain their spot atop the existing American political hierarchy.

But Americans don't all need to agree on a linear, objective story about the proper role of language, culture, and assimilation to support bilingual ballots. Even if Arnold Palmer detests bilingual schools and thinks Congress should adopt English as the official language of the United States, he should support language assistance at the polls. Voting is different.[4]

Why? Because bilingual ballots advance citizen engagement and integration rather than cultural separatism. Prior to the provision for language assistance, many citizens with limited English skills went unregistered because they could not read registration applications or ballots or talk with poll workers. Rather than reach out to citizens who spoke little English, candidates and political parties excluded them and ignored their political interests, which in turn made them feel even less a part of the system. Vilma Martinez, president and general counsel of the Mexican American Legal Defense and Educational Fund, testified before Congress in 1974 that election officials in Uvalde County, Texas, refused to name Latinos as deputy registrars, removed registered Latino voters from voting rolls, and refused to aid Spanish speakers who spoke little English. Others testified that as recently as the early 1970s, native-born Mexican Americans attended segregated schools that denied instruction in English—a situation that served as a structural barrier to participation to many. The enactment of the language-assistance provisions of the Voting Rights Act in 1975, however, sparked voter-registration drives of Latinos. Bilingual ballots gave politicians, parties, and other political groups greater incentives to reach out and form coalitions with language minorities. Perhaps to the dismay of more radical multiculturalists, this informal, voluntary social interaction promotes integration and perhaps even—dare one say it—English.

As Congressman Hamilton Fish, Jr., then the ranking Republican on the U.S. House Judiciary Committee, said in 1992, "[I]t seems evident to me that by enabling language minority citizens to vote in an effective and informed manner, we are giving them a stake in our society, and this assistance provides true access to government that I trust will lead to more, not less integration and inclusion of these citizens in our mainstream." Congressman Fish's insight is not new. During and after the Revolutionary War, the Continental Congress unified Americans by issuing government publications such as the Articles of Confederation in official English, German, and French editions.

Yet English-only advocates assert that immigrants use translations in daily life as a crutch to avoid learning English. For the sake of argument, let's assume that the state's proper role is to select and promote one language—English—over others. The "crutch" argument might seem persuasive regarding policies such as education, since children attend school roughly 180 days a year. Voting, however, occurs only a couple of times a year, is voluntary, and doesn't provide the same incentives to learn English. Those who oppose bilingual ballots also make the unsubstantiated assumption that immigrants need additional incentives to develop their English skills. "This is not just an issue of whether immigrants want to learn English," says Rosalind Gold, the senior director of policy for the National Association of Latino Elected and Appointed Officials (NALEO). "They do. They understand learning English is a part of economic mobility in this country." The negligible benefits of promoting fluency through English-only ballots do not outweigh the significant costs of disenfranchisement and political isolation of language minorities.

In response, bilingual critics might assert that English-only ballots send an important message. According to their argument, English-only ballots convey to newcomers that our nation's most precious collective activity—voting—is conducted in English. Or, in the words of U.S. English's former communications director Jim Lubinskas, "Bilingual ballots are un-American."

But a rejection of bilingual ballots also sends a message: exclusion. Historical discrimination in immigration policies, segregated schools, and other policies have hindered Asian-American and

Latino political influence. Bilingual ballots announce that those days are behind us and that all citizens are valued and have equal standing before the law.

Language assistance at the polls also differs from other multilingual policies because voting raises unique issues of representation. Latinos and Asian Americans are the fastest-growing ethnic groups in the United States; both are increasing at a rate nearly four times that of the total population. Although the Office of Immigration Statistics tracks naturalization rates by country of origin rather than by ethnicity, countries in Asia and the Pacific Islands accounted for 42.1 percent of all newly naturalized U.S. citizens in 2003, and 34.1 percent of all new citizens came from Mexico, Central and South America, and the Caribbean. This means significant numbers of new eligible voters from these ethnic groups. Latinos jumped from 2 percent of the electorate in 1992 to 8 percent in 2004. As demographics change, it is not implausible that a few politicians could exclude newcomers to hang onto power and dictate policy. Bilingual ballots send the message that the government is operating in good faith and is not gaming the system to favor the old guard by suppressing votes among citizens whose English is not as strong.

Critics of bilingual ballots also argue that those with poor English skills are likely to make uninformed decisions at the polls, which in turn produces weaker public policy. Most news broadcasts, newspapers, and political advertisements appear in English, and Americans with minimal English skills thus have less access to important public-affairs information. But Congress rejected the "informed voter" argument in 1965, when it passed Voting Rights Act provisions that banned literacy tests. Even though widespread literacy (like widespread English proficiency) was and continues to be an important goal, illiterate citizens pay taxes, abide by rules, and make other important contributions to society, and we decided they should have a say in our democracy. The same logic applies to those with limited English skills.

Further, the underlying premise that those who speak languages other than English are uninformed is flawed—especially in areas with large numbers of newspapers, radio stations, and even television networks that disseminate local, state, and national news in languages other than English. This is especially true in communities where the language-minority population is significant enough to trigger the Voting Rights Act's language-assistance requirements. Between 2000 and 2005, for example, NBC's Telemundo Spanish television stations increased their average ratings in Chicago by 94 percent, Houston by 100 percent, New York by 184 percent, and Miami by 258 percent.

Political participation by a broad group of Americans—including those with low English proficiency—allows for better rather than worse government decisions. Such participation exposes elected officials to diverse viewpoints and allows them to distribute resources and burdens to reflect evolving problems and needs.[5]

DO BILINGUAL BALLOTS HELP?

Critics also claim that bilingual ballots are unnecessary. English-only proponent Robert Klein Engler, for example, writes:

> [O]ne of the requirements to become a citizen of the United States is the ability to speak English. . . . Because only citizens can vote in United States elections, and because to be a naturalized citizen you have to read, write and speak English, why would any citizen need help or voting materials in a language other than English?

But millions of U.S.-born citizens have limited English skills and benefit from language assistance in voting. Thousands of members of American Indian tribes live on New Mexico, Arizona, and Utah reservations where English is rarely used. These original Americans have inhabited what is now the United States for thousands of years without the need to prove their English abilities to immigration officials. As mentioned earlier, many native-born Mexican Americans attended segregated schools that denied instruction in English, and Puerto Rican–born citizens who migrated to the mainland may not be proficient in English. Four million native-born Americans who speak Spanish as their primary language are limited in their English proficiency.

A variety of other U.S. citizens may lack perfect English skills. Naturalization law requires that most immigrants applying for citizenship "can read or write simple words and phrases" but says nothing about learning technical election-specific terms absent from daily conversation—such as "straight-party vote," "Chief Justice, Third Court of Appeals District," "electors," or "County Surveyor." Naturalization law does not test for the legalese found on many ballot questions, such as the following from the November 2004 Florida ballot:

> Proposes to amend the State Constitution to provide that an injured claimant who enters into a contingency fee agreement with an attorney in a claim for medical liability is entitled to no less than 70% in the first $250,000.00 in all damages received by the claimant, and 90% of damages in excess of $250,000.00, exclusive of reasonable and customary costs and regardless of the number of defendants. This amendment is intended to be self-executing.

Further, naturalization law makes exceptions to the English requirement for a variety of people, such as those over fifty who have lawfully resided in the United States for twenty years, those over fifty-five who have lawfully resided in the United States for at least fifteen years, and those who have a physical or mental impairment that affects their ability to learn English. In short, bilingual ballots help many with limited English skills feel more comfortable and make better-informed decisions at the polls.

Demographic data confirm the need for bilingual ballots. According to the 2000 U.S. Census, more than eight million Americans age eighteen and over admit to speaking English less than "very well." That's more voting-age citizens than live in Michigan, the eighth-largest state in the country. Of this group, 4.5 million speak a form of Spanish and 1.6 million an Asian or Pacific island language. In a survey of Latinos conducted in Spanish in 1989 and 1990, 77 percent of respondents who spoke Spanish at home used bilingual ballots, and almost 58 percent of those who spoke some or only English at home reported that Spanish ballots helped them vote. In light of the small pool of respondents and the 86 percent increase in the number of foreign-born Latinos in the United States between 1990 and 2000, a contemporary survey might provide a more precise picture that shows an increased need for bilingual ballots today.

A survey of Asian-American voters across eight states on Election Day 2004 found that only 14 percent spoke English as their native language, and 41 percent had limited English proficiency. Nearly one in three Asian-American voters relied on some form of language assistance to vote, and nearly half of all first-time voters needed assistance.

We should also be concerned about already-fragile voter participation among language minorities. Voter participation among Latino and Asian-American citizens trails that of whites by roughly twenty points (67 percent of whites voted in 2004, compared with 60 percent of African Americans, 47 percent of Latinos, and 44 percent of Asian-American citizens). While the vast majority of Latinos and Asian Americans speak English, eliminating bilingual ballots would disproportionately affect language-minority communities and broaden racial disparities in voter participation.[6]

DOLLARS AND CENTS

English-only advocates observe that with U.S. citizens fluent in more than 300 languages, language assistance at the polls wastes millions in tax dollars. But the Voting Rights Act is sensitive to costs in that it requires language assistance only in those areas with the greatest need. The federal law requires that an area provide language assistance if it falls under one of two categories that I'll only generally sketch out here: (1) the area has more than 10,000 voting-age citizens or 5 percent of voting-age citizens who speak a single foreign language and do not speak English well enough to participate in the electoral process, or (2) the area in 1972 provided election materials only in English, while having a single language-minority group that accounted for more than 5 percent of voting-age citizens and had voter registration or participation rates of less than 50 percent. Due to the law, some entire states—such as New Mexico and Texas—must provide language assistance in Spanish for statewide elections. Across the United States, more than 490 areas must provide language assistance. Spanish accounts for many of these areas, followed by American Indian/Alaskan Native languages, and then Asian languages.[7]

Critics of bilingual ballots point to the tiny town of Briny Breezes, Florida—population 411—to try to illustrate the unnecessary costs of the Voting Rights Act. Briny Breezes, a trailer park that was incorporated as a city in 1963, is largely a community of senior citizens, 99 percent of whom speak English "very well." The town sits in Palm Beach County, however, which has more than 22,000 Spanish-speaking U.S. citizens with limited English skills and is covered by the language assistance provisions. When Briny Breezes called off its election in 2004 pursuant to Florida state law because no challengers filed to run, it spent $19.65 to translate its announcement into Spanish.

"We have 37 municipalities, and there are a lot of very tiny ones that there's nobody [speaking] Spanish in there," Palm Beach County Supervisor of Elections Theresa LePore told the *Palm Beach Post*. "The feds don't care." (As discussed in chapter 2, LePore is better known for designing the infamous Palm Beach "butterfly" ballot that caused thousands to vote erroneously for Pat Buchanan instead of Al Gore in 2000.) U.S. English announced in a press release that "Briny Breezes has gotten caught up in the ugly tentacles of the Voting Rights Act."

These criticisms muddy the waters because the Voting Rights Act reels in only the most ravenous predators. In less colorful (but perhaps clearer) English, Briny Breezes was not required to spend the $19.65 under the Voting Rights Act because the law does not require language assistance in areas with few voters who have limited English skills. According to the Justice Department, a covered locality need not give bilingual assistance to "all persons or registered voters," but rather may target its efforts so that "language minority group members who need minority language materials and assistance receive them." In short, under the terms of federal law, Briny Breezes did not need to provide bilingual election materials to every resident. In fact, the town probably did not need to provide them at all.

In those areas covered by the Voting Rights Act, studies show that language assistance accounts for less than 5 percent of the cost of elections on average. Many areas are unable to segregate bilingual election costs, but twenty-eight cities and counties that responded to a 1997 federal government survey provided their total bilingual costs for the 1996 election. The expenses varied widely. Central Falls, Rhode Island, for example, reported $100 in printing costs for Spanish materials used at nine polling places (just over $11 per poll). Los Angeles County, California, reported costs of $1.1 million to provide language assistance in Spanish, Chinese, Vietnamese, Japanese, and Tagalog at more than 5,600 polling places ($196 per poll). On average, bilingual election costs were $262 per polling place covered. In dividing the costs of language assistance among all voters in a covered area, localities spent forty-three cents per voter to provide a ballot that reflects the major languages in the community.

In 2005, former Justice Department lawyer Dr. James Tucker and Arizona State University political science professor Dr. Rodolfo Espino released the results of the most comprehensive analysis of language assistance at the polls. Tucker and Espino, along with a team of ten Arizona State University students, worked for eighteen months to compile the study of election officials in 31 states and 361 localities covered by the language-assistance provisions of the Voting Rights Act. Fifty-nine percent of jurisdictions reported no additional costs in providing oral language assistance, and 54.2 percent reported no additional costs for bilingual language written materials. For most areas with additional costs, oral language assistance represented only about 1.5 percent of total election costs and written language materials accounted for only 3 percent of such costs.

Through responsible administration, states and localities can contain costs. According to a 1997 federal study, 82 percent of areas covered by the Voting Rights Act had bilingual employees in their offices or at the polls to assist voters, 15 percent used volunteer assistants, and only 13 percent hired special interpreters to provide language assistance. The pool of bilingual individuals is often sufficiently broad in localities covered by the Voting Rights Act to hire bilingual election office clerks and recruit poll workers.

Bilingual poll workers represent zero cost when they receive the same pay as other poll workers, although some counties do supplement their pay. Many areas use county employees, who generally provide a high level of performance, are easily trainable, and are familiar with county practices and guidelines. Clark County, Nevada, for example, uses county personnel in every polling place—regardless of language skill—in order to maintain high-quality poll workers. Counties also work with local high schools and colleges to establish programs in which students can serve as poll workers as part of an educational exercise. The student works, gets paid, writes a paper, participates in democracy, and receives academic credit. Further, many counties reach out to local community organizations that work with language minorities, and these community groups sometimes help recruit bilingual poll workers or adopt particular polling places to provide language assistance.

The Justice Department is also interested in minimizing cost and avoiding waste, such as publishing Spanish notices in English newspapers. Officials allow flexibility in the mode of publication and encourage counties to build information trees of all people and groups with e-mail. That way, they can send bilingual information to hundreds of groups, asking them to post information on listservs or make announcements at community meetings—all at essentially zero cost. Some counties find it to be an administrative convenience to provide a bilingual package at every polling location, although having bilingual personnel to provide oral assistance at every site is very rare.

In 2004, Ventura County, California, learned to be frugal the hard way when the U.S. Justice Department charged that it had failed to provide enough bilingual poll workers and voting materials. With more than 33 percent of the county's population being Latino, it has 26,000 Spanish-speaking U.S. citizens with limited English skills. The county settled the matter by agreeing to provide its first Spanish-language ballot.

In an attempt to drum up bilingual poll workers, Ventura officials offered county employees the day off with pay plus a stipend of $60 to $90. About 150 county employees volunteered, most of whom were bilingual, thus ensuring that 300 of the county's 1,300 poll workers would speak both Spanish and English. "It was an opportunity for county employees to lend a hand, and we had a tremendous response," said county Assistant Registrar Gene Browning.

County employees at the polls worked from 6 A.M. to 9 P.M. (almost doubling their work day), and many volunteered for reasons other than the extra money. "I want people to feel comfortable going to vote," Public Health Department employee Letty Alvarez told the *Los Angeles Times*, "and I think they will be more likely to vote if there is a friendly face there to offer encouragement." Eight-year county employee Elizabeth Taylor volunteered to staff a polling place at a local elementary school. "I am an immigrant and I think this is an opportunity to demonstrate to this country my gratitude," said Taylor. "Doing this work makes me feel very proud."

In addition to reaching out to their own employees and inclusively hiring and recruiting volunteers, counties and cities can take other steps to contain costs. According to a 1997 federal study, 95 percent of localities and 85 percent of states that provide language assistance used bilingual ballots (a single ballot in English that also has a translation) rather than separate translated ballots, thus lowering the printing costs. Recent developments in touch-screen electronic-voting-machine technology have further reduced the costs of translated materials.

One of the top 100 questions that the U.S. Citizenship and Immigration Services asks potential citizens is: "What is the most important right granted to U.S. citizens?" The proper answer is "The right to vote."[8] If our government finds the right to vote the epitome of citizenship, how can we justify denying citizens that right because of lesser skills in English?

LOST IN TRANSLATION

In the early 1990s, up to 70 percent of residents in New York's Chinatown spoke little English. Only about 30 percent of eligible Chinatown voters were registered. Although New York City had over a half-million residents of Asian ancestry, not one had ever been elected to city, state, or federal office. In 1992, when Congress expanded the Voting Rights Act's language-assistance requirements to include localities with 10,000 citizens who speak a single foreign language, New York City added Chinese voting materials and oral assistance. By 1996, an estimated 30 percent of Chinese-American voters in the city relied on the Chinese ballots. The total cost for providing Chinese- and Spanish-language assistance accounted for just under 4 percent of the city's total $16 million election budget.

In November 2000, Chinese Americans in New York City voted in record numbers. But there were mishaps. On Chinese ballots at six polling locations in the borough of Queens, the translations for the party headings for state races were transposed. "Republican" was translated as "Democratic," and "Democratic" as "Republican." On the absentee ballot, the Chinese directions for the state Supreme Court justice contest first told voters to "Vote for any FIVE," and then directed them to "Vote for any THREE" (the English ballot read, "Vote for any THREE"). At a school polling site, election officials arranged for five Chinese interpreters but only one appeared. Other sites ran out of Chinese-language voting materials. The Board of Elections had to provide magnifying glasses for reading Chinese ballots because the character type was so small. "The Board of Elections has been careless," Asian American Legal Defense and Education Fund (AALDEF) Executive Director Margaret Fung told the *Village Voice*. "This is just inexcusable."

The New York City Board of Elections had contracted with a New Jersey company, Global Word, Inc., to translate its ballots. An account manager at Global Word, Alan Bertelle, claimed that the company relied on the elections board to point out errors. But the board had a different understanding. "We rely on the accuracy of our translation companies," board spokesperson Naomi Bernstein told the *Village Voice*, adding that the board has staff members "who are Asian" examine the ballots. Board of Elections clerk Matt Graves clarified that the city has "employees that have Chinese language skills that read it, but there is no one employed to do it. It's based on a sight comparison."

Based on stories like those related to the 2000 New York City election, critics claim that bilingual ballots are often inaccurate and confusing. The persons providing oral assistance may have a partisan agenda that goes undetected by other poll workers who speak only English. Even when translators have good motives, translation is "far from an exact science." Ballot-initiative and referendum questions are often written in complex legal language that is difficult to understand even in English, and other languages may not have English-equivalent words.

But it is unclear whether the percentage of errors, fraud, or partisan abuse is higher with bilingual ballots and workers than with those that are English-only. Stories of partisanship or incompetence regarding ballots emerge from many elections, such as Palm Beach's confusing "butterfly" ballot. While errors on non-English election materials may not be caught if few election officials read and speak the specific language, the fact that most translators carefully focus on clarity and accuracy might result in fewer mistakes on bilingual ballots than on English-only ones. Outside of anecdotes, we need better evidence that the pervasiveness of error and fraud is considerably higher with bilingual ballots than with English ballots. Even then, English-only advocates must show that the probability of error is so high with bilingual ballots that it outweighs the likelihood that Americans with limited English ability will either misinterpret English-only ballots or simply not vote.

Also, initial translation difficulties with languages such as Chinese do not mean that the error rate is high for languages with which a city has had more experience, such as Spanish. "We've never had a problem with Spanish in a thousand years," Daniel De Francesco, executive director of the New York City elections board, told the *Village Voice*. "We have staff members that speak Spanish." Simply because New York City invested insufficient resources in hiring Chinese-speaking staff and monitoring the accuracy of translations does not mean it should not or will not invest sufficient resources in the future. A central purpose of the Voting Rights Act language-assistance requirements is to ensure that localities invest resources so that those with limited English skills can cast a ballot. Translation may "seem like Greek" in the beginning, but with sufficient dedication and experience, states and localities can do it.

If anyone would be overwhelmed by various languages at the polls, it might be Los Angeles County Registrar-Recorder/County Clerk Conny McCormack. The county provides ballots in more languages than any other area in the nation—including English, Chinese, Japanese, Korean, Spanish, Tagalog, and Vietnamese. Of about 22,000 poll workers in the county leading up to the 2004 election, almost 5,000 said they were bilingual. Nonetheless, McCormack declared that anyone with poor English skills could bring a translator to the polls. "The goal is for everyone to be able to vote," McCormack said.[9]

WHY DON'T BILINGUAL-BALLOT REQUIREMENTS APPLY TO ALL NON-ENGLISH LANGUAGES?

Imagine, for example, that an enclave of Russian immigrants develops in Brighton Beach, a community in the Coney Island section of Brooklyn, New York. The enclave has 20,000 U.S. citizens whose primary language is Russian and whose English skills are limited. Currently, the Voting Rights Act requires language assistance only for Spanish and for American Indian, Asian-American, and Alaskan Native languages. Should the Voting Rights Act be expanded to include Russian, Haitian (French Creole), Brazilian (Portuguese),

Middle Eastern (Arabic), and other language communities? Indeed, critics of bilingual ballots might assert that if these groups have limited English skills and satisfy the population thresholds in a city or county (10,000 or 5 percent of voting-age U.S. citizens), the Voting Rights Act should guarantee access to bilingual ballots. We should either provide bilingual ballots for all groups or not provide them at all, critics sometimes argue.

In light of the value of bilingual ballots, I would agree in principle that they should be provided to any group that needs them. The Voting Rights Act's language-assistance requirements are not more expansive, however, because of the "states'-rights" arguments I explained in chapter 2. In short, even though the court decisions are murky, the federal government probably can require bilingual ballots in all languages for federal elections, but it probably can mandate bilingual ballots for state and local offices only for those groups that have experienced discrimination at the polls. Congress originally limited the language-assistance provisions to protect Spanish, and American Indian, Asian-American, and Alaskan Native languages, due to the record of past and current discrimination against speakers of these languages provided during hearings. To the extent that other groups are systematically excluded and can satisfy the states'-rights hurdle, the Voting Rights Act's language-assistance requirements should be expanded to include them. If not, counties and localities should on their own—as a matter of good democratic practice—provide bilingual materials and assistance when needed.

Latinos, Asian Americans, Native Americans, and Alaskan Natives should not be perceived as well-organized interest groups vying for a larger slice of the political pie while ignoring needed voting protections to other language minorities. The technical requirement of states' rights, which has traditionally hindered such other congressional reforms as expansion of voting to eighteen-year-olds, is the true culprit.

While the Voting Rights Act should provide language assistance only for groups that can establish evidence of discrimination because of federalism concerns, the language provisions might be modified in other ways. For example, Congress should clarify federal regulations that allow localities to target their language-assistance efforts. On the one hand, a county should not fail to provide language assistance in neighborhoods that have a significant number of language minorities just because the county "interprets" targeting too narrowly. On the other hand, we don't want a county to waste valuable language-assistance resources and local funds at polling locations where they will not be used. Clarifying and publicizing targeting guidelines so that counties and cities better understand how to use their resources most efficiently will go a long way toward enhancing compliance. It might also correct the misguided assumption that the Voting Rights Act requires language assistance in small towns where the primary language of 99 percent of voters is English.

Whether or not Congress tinkers at the margins of the Voting Rights Act, it should preserve the bilingual-ballot and language-assistance provisions. Because of the value of widespread participation and the dangers of entrenchment unique to democracy, bilingual ballots raise issues that do not exist in the typical debate between multiculturalism and assimilation. What better way to convey the meaning of citizenship than to give citizens access to the voting booth?

Unfortunately, citizens' access to voting is also threatened by "antifraud" advocates who have yet to prove that their proposals will prevent even one fraudulent voter for every thousand legitimate voters excluded.

CHAPTER SIX

FRAUD OR SUPPRESSION?

In 2003, the Republican-controlled South Dakota legislature instigated a photo-identification requirement for the first time. It so happened that a few months earlier, South Dakota's 16,000 Democratic-leaning American Indian voters carried U.S. Senate candidate Tim Johnson to a narrow 524-vote victory over a Republican challenger. Voters now have to show poll workers a South Dakota driver's license, a state-issued photo ID, a tribal photo ID, or a state university photo ID.

Supporters of the photo ID requirement insisted that the law was necessary to prevent voter fraud, and alleged that fraudulent registrations came from American Indian areas in the 2002 contest. "The tradition in South Dakota is that we carefully protect the right to vote," claimed Republican State Representative Stan Adelstein, chairman of the State–Tribal Relations Committee. Pennington County Auditor Julie Pearson explained the law this way: "People wanted to be assured they would be allowed to vote their vote. If someone votes your name prior to you getting there, you are the one who doesn't get to vote. Without an ID law, there is nothing auditors can do to assure that to voters or to the courts."

But opponents discounted the threat of fraud and asserted that the photo-ID requirement disproportionately harmed American Indians. "What was broke in South Dakota that required us to pass this legislation? In my opinion, there was nothing broken," said Thomas Shortbull, president of Oglala Lakota College on the Pine Ridge Reservation and a former South Dakota state senator. Tom Katus, a member of the Northern Plains Tribal Voter Education Project, claimed: "I've never seen anyone in my life double-vote. The law should never have been there. . . . The Legislature over-reached, and this thing should be thrown out."

According to Oliver Semans, an activist and an enrolled member of the Rosebud Sioux, "The people of the Rosebud Sioux Indian Reservation, 99 percent of them, know that this law was put in place to suppress their vote and punish them for 2002." Many American Indians in South Dakota do not drive cars and lack driver's licenses. Several tribes do not issue photo-identification cards. Semans said that the new law "is basically telling [American Indians] that we don't trust you. That's the message."

Defenders of the photo-ID requirement claimed that the law was not intended to discriminate against American Indians, and they emphasized that the law provided that even those without a photo ID could vote if they simply signed an affidavit confirming their identity. Indeed, data from the first election covered by the new law in June 2004 confirmed suspicions that a disproportionately large number of American Indian voters did not bring photo IDs to the polls, and that if the affidavit option had not been available, they would not have been allowed to vote. Affidavits were signed by under 2 percent of voters statewide, but in each of the predominantly American Indian counties (Shannon, Todd, Corson, Dewey, and Ziebach), 5.3 to 16 percent of voters signed affidavits.

But not everyone who arrived at the polls without a photo ID during the June 2004 election was given the opportunity to sign an affidavit. Yankton Sioux tribal elder Edna Weddell went to vote without a photo ID. When Ms. Weddell's granddaughter asked that

Ms. Weddell be allowed to sign an affidavit, the poll worker refused. Ms. Weddell, who uses a walker, eventually did vote, but only after returning home to retrieve her ID. Written poll worker instructions in Corson County even stated: "Some voters are reporting that ID is not required. Please inform the voters that ID is in fact required." There was no mention of providing affidavits.

South Dakota Secretary of State Chris Nelson, a Republican, acknowledged that some poll workers did not offer voters who arrived without IDs the opportunity to fill out an affidavit, and he promised better compliance in the future by the state's 3,500 poll workers. But he stood by the ID provision, noting that many who were not offered affidavits returned to their cars or homes to get a photo ID. "The ultimate question is, is it too much to ask that each person placing a ballot in our ballot box is who they say they are?" he said.

"That's not the question," responded Jennifer Ring, executive director of the American Civil Liberties Union of the Dakotas. "The question is, is this a reasonable and fair way for the state to address that?" Rosebud Sioux member Oliver Semans elaborated: "The law you put into effect to stop one person from doing something wrong in turn affects hundreds or thousands who have done nothing wrong. You are punishing thousands for what you think might happen."[1]

FRAUD OR ACCESS

The conflicting values of voter integrity and voter access increasingly frame today's debates about democracy. Often, measures that prevent fraud in elections—such as photo-ID requirements—make voting more difficult and reduce access for legitimate voters.

Republicans often claim that voter fraud represents a primary threat to democracy. They call for measures that enhance integrity in the electoral process, such as photo-ID requirements, partisan challenges to the qualifications of particular voters, purges of voter rolls, and rigorous requirements for registering to vote. Drawing on historical images of Democratic big-city political machines stuffing ballot boxes with votes of dead people, integrity advocates claim voting has become too easy. They warn that legitimate votes are diluted by fraudulent ballots cast by felons, migrant farmworkers, terrorists, and homeless people who vote multiple times in exchange for cigarettes and cash.

Democrats, on the other hand, often prioritize widespread access to voting. They claim that the call for increased voter integrity serves as a pretext to create barriers that disproportionately exclude people of color and less-affluent voters.

In October 2002, U.S. Attorney General John Ashcroft launched a "Voter Access and Integrity Project," which emphasized the role of the Justice Department's Civil Rights Division in eradicating discriminatory barriers and the Public Integrity Section's role in preventing voter fraud. In 2002, Congress passed the Help America Vote Act, which enhances access by providing provisional ballots to registered voters whose names do not appear on the rolls. But the law also appeased the integrity hawks by requiring all first-time voters who registered by mail to provide idenification when they arrive at the polls.

In his book *Stealing Elections: How Voter Fraud Threatens Our Democracy*, *Wall Street Journal* editor John Fund offers perhaps the most comprehensive statement of the emerging integrity movement. According to Fund, in 2001 the voter rolls of many American cities contained more names than the U.S. Census listed as the total number of voting-age residents. He writes of fictitious people and pets being registered and cites examples of political operatives giving homeless people cigarettes and cash to cast a vote. Fund asserts that the National Voter Registration Act ("Motor Voter Act"):

. . . imposed fraud-friendly rules on the states by requiring driver's license bureaus to register anyone applying for licenses, to offer mail-in registration with no identification needed, and to forbid government workers to challenge new registrants, while making it difficult to purge "deadwood" voters (those who have died or moved away).

According to Fund, prosecutions for voter fraud are rare because prosecutors fear "charges of racism or of a return to Jim Crow voter suppression tactics if they pursue touchy fraud cases."

Fund proposes that a photo-ID requirement at the polls and more vigorous prosecutions would prevent fraud. Other voting-integrity advocates, such as Hans A. von Spakovsky, a member of the Federal Election Commission, add that the presence of partisan challengers at the polls also prevents voter fraud.

But antifraud proponents make their claims without answering vital questions. For example, what is the evidence of massive, widespread fraud? Do voter-integrity proposals disproportionately burden less-affluent voters or voters of color? Since conservatives are generally skeptical of regulation due to their distrust of big government, how do they ensure that politicians don't manipulate political outcomes by adopting antifraud regulations that suppress participation by legitimate voters? Have voter-integrity proponents established that their proposals, when enacted, will exclude fewer legitimate voters than fraudulent voters?

WHO TAKES THE HIT?

Proponents of antifraud measures such as photo-ID requirements fail to undertake a serious cost-benefit analysis. While more research is needed, the existing evidence suggests that the harm of a photo-ID requirement would seriously outweigh any speculative benefit. Indeed, antifraud activists cannot establish that a photo-ID requirement would exclude even one fraudulent vote for every thousand eligible voters excluded.

According to the 2001 Carter-Ford Commission, an estimated 6 percent to 10 percent of voting-age Americans (up to 19 million potential voters) do not possess a driver's license or a state-issued nondriver's photo ID. A photo-ID requirement would exclude Americans of all backgrounds, but the poor, the disabled, the elderly, students, and people of color would bear the greatest burden. According to the Georgia chapter of AARP, 36 percent of Georgians over age seventy-five do not have a driver's license. In the United States, more than 3 million people with disabilities do not have identification issued by the government. A June 2005 study in Wisconsin found that the rate of driver's license possession among African Americans was half of that for whites. Among men ages eighteen to twenty-four, 36 percent of whites, 57 percent of Latinos, and 78 percent of African Americans lacked a valid driver's license. A series of factors may explain these disparities, including that fewer people of color and fewer poor Americans own automobiles or are willing to pay the fee required to obtain a state ID card.[2]

Even if cash-strapped governments agreed to issue photo IDs to those without driver's licenses free of charge, there would still be the financial burden of providing the underlying documentation to obtain that "free" ID. A certified copy of a birth certificate costs from $10 to $45 depending on the state, a passport costs $85, and certified naturalization papers cost $19.95. Even aside from the cost and the paperwork, limited business hours, long lines, and other factors prevent many state DMV offices from being easily accessible models of efficiency. For example, in 2005 only one of the ten Georgia counties with the highest percentage of blacks had an office that issued state IDs, and no such office existed in Atlanta. When faced with the prospect of spending hours away from work, family, and other obligations to secure a photo ID used a couple of times a year to vote, many citizens will unfortunately choose to forgo their vote.

The exclusionary effects of a photo-ID requirement are best illustrated by some of the people it is most likely to disenfranchise—the victims of Hurricane Katrina. Many who were left behind in hurricane-torn New Orleans were poor, did not own a car, and were less likely to have a driver's license. These forgotten Americans—and many like them across our nation—are the ones a photo-ID requirement would most likely leave out of our democracy.

While a photo-ID requirement would exclude millions of voters, antifraud activists have failed to prove that it would prevent more than a few fraudulent votes. Instead, photo-ID proponents try to bolster their claims by citing fraud that would not be prevented by a photo-ID. For example, rather than grappling with the extent to which antifraud measures suppress voter participation, John Fund suggests that fraud hurts not only white candidates but also candidates of color. He reports that Latino Congressman Ciro Rodriguez lost a Democratic primary when a "missing ballot box appeared in south Texas with enough votes to make his opponent the Democratic nominee by 58 votes." But Fund creates a straw man. If we assume that the missing ballot box was filled with illegitimate votes, then Congressman Rodriguez seems to have been defeated by fraud committed by election administrators rather than fraudulent voters. Antifraud measures designed to monitor election workers would have been more effective in protecting the Rodriguez election than photo-ID requirements or regular purges of voting rolls that could dampen the political influence of legitimate Latino voters.

Other proponents of photo ID generally invoke anecdotes of fraud to support their claims, but generally their examples do not justify a photo-ID requirement. For example, a photo-ID requirement at the polls does nothing to prevent fraud by absentee voting. Nor does it prevent voting by ineligible persons with felony convictions who are misinformed of their voting rights. Rather, a photo-ID requirement guards against only one type of fraud: individuals arriving at the polls to vote using false information, such as the name of another registered voter or a recent but not current address. These are extraordinarily inefficient means to influence the results of an election. Since the costs of this form of fraud are extremely high (federal law provides for up to five years' imprisonment), and the benefits to any individual voter are extremely low, it is highly unlikely that this will ever occur with any frequency.

In the most comprehensive survey of alleged election fraud to date, Professor Loraine Minnite and David Callahan have shown that the incidence of individual voter fraud at the polls is negligible. A few prominent examples support their findings. In Ohio, a statewide survey found four instances of ineligible persons voting or attempting to vote in 2002 and 2004, out of 9,078,728 votes cast—a rate of 0.00004%. In 2005, Georgia Secretary of State Cathy Cox stated that she could not recall one documented case of voter fraud relating to the impersonation of a registered voter at the polls during her ten-year tenure as secretary of state or assistant secretary of state. An extensive investigation in Washington state following the 2004 election uncovered less than one case of double voting or voting in the name of another for every 100,000 ballots cast.

John Fund points to the potential for fraud from dead or otherwise inactive or ineligible voters left on voter registration lists. While such fraud is rare, it is addressed by the Help America Vote Act's provisions that require regular cleaning of the registration lists to remove persons rendered ineligible by felony conviction or death. Once HAVA's provisions are implemented, persons who have been rendered ineligible by a felony conviction or death will simply not be listed on the voter rolls as eligible voters. Thus, if such persons—or others purporting to be them—show up at the polls, they will not be able to cast a regular ballot.

While existing facts suggest that individual election fraud that would be deterred by photo ID is extremely rare, there is hard evidence that a photo-ID requirement would unduly burden millions of eligible voters who lack ID. Photo-ID advocates argue that in a close election a small amount of fraud could make the margin of difference. It is equally true, however, that the rejection of a much larger number of eligible voters could make a much bigger difference in the outcome. Based on the existing evidence, the exclusion of legitimate voters through restrictive photo-ID requirements are likely to erroneously determine the outcome of thousands of more elections than any speculative fraud by individual voters at the polls.[3]

THE BENEFITS OF EXCLUDING VOTERS

Antifraud advocates argue that responsible individuals who properly register and bring a photo ID to the polls have nothing to fear from their proposed regulations. They assert that those who want to vote will take the steps required to meet eligibility standards. Indeed, the argument goes, isn't it paternalistic to assume that people of color and the poor are too irresponsible to obtain a photo ID?

Many Americans accept these justifications at face value. Why shouldn't they? I always carry my driver's license in my wallet when I leave home. This isn't a big deal, one might think.

But politicians see things differently. They focus much of their time and mental energy on activities that will get them reelected or will increase their political influence—activities such as raising money and attracting media attention. With similar intensity, politicians fixate on understanding who goes to the polls and how to ensure a political mix that provides them with a safe margin of victory and maximizes their party's influence. Politicians know that a slight reduction in the ballots cast by minority or poorer voters can determine who controls the governor's mansion, the U.S. Senate, or even the White House.

Voter-integrity advocates emphasize the steps a person can take to protect the *individual* right to vote, but they fail to address the *structural* impact of self-interested politicians who champion such rules in order to manipulate political outcomes. By making it more difficult to register and vote, voter-integrity rules allow politicians to modulate and control the electorate. And it is not just poor and minority voters who are harmed. Antifraud regulations that hinder voter access allow politicians to pander to a narrowly defined group of experienced likely voters, with less fear that discontented new voters will enter the electorate and support a candidate who challenges the status quo. In 1998, Minnesota's same-day registration—which is opposed by many voter-integrity proponents—allowed 250,000 new voters to mobilize around and elect as governor political newcomer Jesse Ventura, who won by under 57,000 votes. Supporters of a variety of candidates who challenge the establishment—such as Democrats Howard Dean and Al Sharpton, as well as Republicans Gary Bauer and Pat Robertson—face disadvantages when they confront heightened hurdles. Voter-integrity regulations are framed as necessary to protect the votes of regular Americans, but they can actually exclude many Americans from the political process and entrench incumbents.

Voter-integrity advocates claim that photo-ID requirements for voting are reasonable because individuals now must produce photo identification to board airplanes, use a credit card, or buy liquor and cigarettes. But voting differs from air travel, check cashing, and entering federal buildings. Airlines, for example, have no incentives to exclude legitimate travelers, while some politicians have incentives to exclude legitimate voters who are likely to cast ballots for their opponents (as we see in the redistricting context). An individual air traveler or credit-card user is inconvenienced by having forgotten to carry on ID; with voting, however, the harm extends past an absentminded voter and impinges upon political allies and a democracy that fails to reflect the will of the people.

Supporters of voter IDs argue that several other nations in the world use voter IDs. But most of the established democracies with which we usually compare the United States—such as the United Kingdom, Australia, Canada, Ireland, New Zealand, Sweden, and Denmark—do not require identification as a condition of voting. A few established democracies that require identification for voting do so only in special circumstances. Germany, for instance, requires identification only of those voters who do not furnish their "notice of polling" or who appear to vote in a polling place other than that in which they are registered. "[E]stablished democracies are less likely to require voters to identify themselves other than verbally," write Professors Louis Massicotte, André Blais, and Antoine Yoshinaka in their book *Establishing the Rules of the Game: Election Laws in Democracies*. "Non-established democracies probably worry more about electoral fraud."[4]

Further, many other nations do not have the same embarrassingly low voter-participation rate as the United States, and a photo-ID requirement threatens to further depress American turnout. In many elections in the United States, less than half of the eligible population participates, ensuring that our nation trails many others in voter turnout by twenty to thirty points (the United States ranks 139th out of 172 democracies in voter participation). This is in part because many other nations do not place the burden to register on individual citizens; they place the burden of universal registration for all citizens on the government. As a result, whereas an estimated 70 percent of eligible American citizens are registered, the number is as high as 94 percent in Mexico. In the United States, a photo-ID requirement would further depress participation and ensure that our government does not reflect the will of all Americans.

Finally, most other nations do not have the extensive local control that characterizes U.S. elections. Such local administration allows for nonuniform and sometimes biased application of a photo-ID requirement by poll workers—some voters may be asked while others may not.

Some might claim that election outcomes should not be shaped by the votes of those "too irresponsible" to take a photo ID to the polls or flawlessly complete a detailed voter-registration form. But what are the limits on such logic? Can a relatively secular blue state bar voting by born-again Evangelicals because faith "clouds" their reasoning in the voting booth? Can a majority-Christian red state block voting by gays? Even when voter-integrity advocates do not explicitly acknowledge their desire to silence some Americans, many of their regulations are not content-neutral. Both Republicans and Democrats suspect that people of color and poorer Americans disproportionately lack photo IDs and that these groups vote predominantly Democratic. Even politicians with good-faith concerns about voter integrity often discount the costs of their proposed antifraud rules because of the political ideology of legitimate voters most likely to be excluded.

Restrictions purporting to prevent voters from cheating also give significant discretion to partisan election administrators who often have greater incentives and opportunities to rig elections than voters. In anticipation of the 2004 election, Florida Republican Secretary of State Glenda Hood—who was appointed by governor Jeb Bush and campaigned in 2000 for George W. Bush—implemented an aggressive campaign to purge the election rolls of felons. (As discussed in chapter 2, Florida and two other states prohibit people who have committed any felony from voting for life, even after they have completed their sentences.) Hood's office compiled a list of "felons" to be omitted from voting rolls and refused to disclose her list to the public. After a court ordered its release, journalists discovered that the list improperly included 2,100 former prisoners who had successfully applied for a restoration of their voting rights. Due to another "computer error," the list included about 22,000 African Americans but only an estimated 61 Latinos—who are much less likely than African Americans to vote Democratic in Florida. The list was scrapped.

The banner of voter integrity allows for abuse in other ways. As mentioned earlier, contrary to South Dakota law, many poll workers failed to give American Indian voters affidavits to verify their identity in lieu of a photo ID. In New York City, which has no photo-ID requirement, a study showed that poll workers illegally asked one in six Asian Americans for identification at the polls. A federal court in Ohio found that during the 2004 presidential election, Republicans deployed their poll monitors so that only 14 percent of new voters in predominantly white precincts would face a Republican challenger, while fully 97 percent of new voters in African-American precincts would face one. Just before the 2004 election, the Board of Registrars in rural Atkinson County, Georgia, sent letters to ninety-six individuals with Spanish surnames—roughly 80 percent of the county's Latino residents—informing them that their right to vote was being challenged. The letters directed the voters to appear at a court hearing five days before the election to present evidence of citizenship if they wanted to contest the matter. Of course, this might mean having to take time from work, which can be problematic if not impossible on short notice. Just before the election, the Board of Registrars declared that the challenges were "legally insufficient because they're based solely on race."[5]

Rather than expressing concern about political abuse, voter-integrity advocates seem to justify profiling at the polls. Although he provides no data or other comprehensive evidence, John Fund writes: "Most fraud is found in urban areas." Fund cites sources explaining that "Republican election fraud is less common," because poorer, inner-city, and minority Democrats have fewer resources and are more susceptible to invitations to participate in voter fraud. Of the eight chapters in *Stealing Elections*, Fund devotes five to fraud among urban residents, undocumented aliens, Latinos, American Indians, and Hawaiians.

Politicians' claims that regulations will enhance voter integrity are appealing, but incumbents throughout history have advanced seemingly benign justifications to benefit themselves. White politicians once argued that poll taxes were necessary to cover the costs of elections and that literacy tests were needed to ensure an intelligent pool of voters. While all of these claims are made to appear plausible at first glance, an informed judgment requires that we consider them in the context of their proponents' political interests.

One anonymous Internet user was more explicit about the need for photo IDs at the polls (I've omitted three characters that were included in the original e-mail address):

> Sep 22, 2004 6:33 pm . . . "Whitey B Pistoff" <Fuc#UNi°°ers@yahoo.com> . . . four nigs are less likely to have an ID, drag your lazy black ass down to a DMV and get an ID . . . in a long drawn out whine Buuutttttt whhhhhhy can't diiiiir- rrrrtttttt bags vote . . . because slowly we are taking back our country that's why

DEVELOPING FAIR ANTIFRAUD RULES

Not all politicians who trumpet the value of voter integrity do so solely for political advantage. But most politicians—whether Republican or Democrat—see these issues through lenses colored by partisan consequences and election prospects, and they use shallow slogans to argue for or against antifraud regulations with little analysis. We should examine whether the benefits of antifraud proposals outweigh the costs.

To do this, we need facts. Beyond a few anecdotes about voter fraud and speculation about how easy it would have been to commit fraud if one were inclined to do so, antifraud activists fail to produce tangible data establishing that the costs of systemic fraud outweigh the costs of their proposals. The U.S. Senate Republican Policy Committee, for example, warned in a February 2005 report: "[V]oter fraud continues to plague our nation's federal elections, diluting and canceling out the votes of the vast majority of Americans." But the report itself fails to establish that more than .001 percent of votes cast are fraudulent, or that more than .001 percent of elections are determined by the ballots of fraudulent voters. Without better data, voter-integrity advocates can easily inflate the threat of fraud, while access advocates can easily discount it.

Perhaps the pervasiveness of voter fraud has not been established because it is evasive. Unlike shoplifting, no missing inventory allows us to measure the precise magnitude of the problem. Nevertheless, random sampling could give us a rough idea of the percentage of votes cast fraudulently. If the antifraud advocates are serious, they should fund unbiased, reliable research. For example, political scientists could contact a statistically representative sampling of 1,000 people who purportedly voted in the last election, ask them if they actually voted, and confirm what percentage of the 1,000 are valid voters. Similarly, researchers could review the closest elections in the country, engage in a random sampling of voters in those elections to estimate the pervasiveness of fraud, and predict how often voter fraud determined the outcome. Researchers could also scour county records for voter fraud allegations and convictions, and the federal government could collect data on voter fraud (just as it collects data on other crimes). No method is perfect, but a serious effort at compiling the extent and types of actual voter fraud will provide more reliable data than a couple of unsubstantiated anecdotes and speculation about the potential for voter fraud.

matching the signature on the voter's absentee ballot against the signature used to register. (I was a member of the commission and dissented. At our last meeting a rule was announced limiting dissent to 250 words, and thus I bought a Web site and posted my full 600-word dissent at www.carterbakerdissent.com). Similarly, in 2005 Georgia reduced its list of acceptable identification from seventeen (including nonphoto ID such as a bank statement, utility bill, or government paycheck) to six forms of state-issued photo ID in an attempt to prevent "fraud." With regard to absentee voting, however, Georgia scrapped its old law that limited absentee voting to people who met narrow requirements such as being age seventy-five and older or disabled, and expanded absentee voting to anyone who applies (absentee voters in Georgia are exempt from photo-ID requirements). The double standard employed by the Carter-Baker Commission and the State of Georgia is particularly disturbing because absentee ballots are widely acknowledged to be more susceptible to fraud than ballots cast at the polls. Further, whites are much more likely than African Americans to vote absentee. Photo-ID advocates fail to explain why Americans who travel to the polls to vote should be denied the same opportunity as absentee voters to establish their identity through signature verification.

In addition to affidavits, there are other safety nets to ensure that those who come to the polls without a photo ID can cast a ballot. Loyola professor Richard Hasen has proposed that counties use biometric systems that contain data on each voter, so that voters who do not bring photo ID to the polls will still be able to vote (although this could raise civil liberties concerns). In *Dirty Little Secrets: The Persistence of Corruption in American Politics*, political scientist Larry J. Sabato and *Wall Street Journal* reporter Glenn R. Simpson recommended that voters provide a thumbprint at the time of registration, which would be digitized and transferred to each precinct so that registered voters could be scanned and cleared to vote when they visit the polls on election day. Ohio State legal bills that drain limited voter-mobilization resources. Thus, antifraud regulations on these organizations should be based on solid data and crafted to be no broader than necessary. We need comprehensive research rather than anecdotes to determine how often voter-mobilization groups actually fill out fake absentee ballots or pay homeless individuals to enter polling locations and vote under assumed names. We should also be open to the possibility that not all fraud by voter-registration groups skews election outcomes. For example, voter-registration workers might earn $2 for every registration collected, and a few bad apples might pad their wallets by inventing registrations for "Mary Poppins" and other fictional persons (this issue also arises when campaigns pay workers to gather signatures for petitions). Studies might find, however, that few of these false registrations result in people who show up at the polls posing as "Mary Poppins" to cast a fraudulent vote, and that the fraud primarily hurts voter-registration organizations and local governments that waste money to register fake people.

The best way to curb fraud by voter-registration and voter-mobilization groups is for the United States to follow many other democracies and adopt universal voter registration. Rather than trying to distinguish fraudulent voter-registration groups from legitimate ones with excessive regulation, states should assume responsibility for registering all eligible individuals to vote. Politicians might be reluctant—because it would diminish their ability to target their registration efforts to doctor the composition of the electorate, and it would mean that any disgruntled group of voters would face fewer hurdles in expressing their frustration at the polls. But universal registration would eliminate concerns about fraud by voter registration groups, and it would have the impact of increasing voter participation. Universal registration is also practical—every high school student who is a U.S. citizen could be automatically registered when he or she turns eighteen, and the government could register the remainder of Americans who are not on the voting rolls during the U.S. census count every ten years.

In analyzing antifraud measures, we must demand answers to important questions. How many legitimate voters will be excluded relative to fraudulent voters? Will the antifraud proposals likely be applied in a uniform way, or will partisans enjoy broad discretion to enforce the proposals selectively? Do the antifraud measures disproportionately exclude legitimate voters who are racial minorities, poor, or members of particular political groups? Can we tailor the proposals so that they remain effective but exclude few legitimate voters? Because some antifraud regulations exclude legitimate voters and skew election outcomes, we should target our antifraud efforts primarily to monitor election administrators, and consider regulating voter-registration and voter-mobilization groups only if studies show high levels of fraud. We should burden voters with antifraud regulations only as a last resort, and even these rules must be narrowly tailored so as not to hinder legitimate voters from casting their ballots.

CONCLUSION

THE CHOICE

Our existing electoral system encourages politicians to maintain power by massaging election rules, district boundaries, and other practices. The Voting Rights Act of 1965, which limits politicians' ability to manipulate democracy unfairly, is under siege. An underfunded, patchwork election system guarantees inequality among voters. For the most part, voters placated by hollow slogans about the "strength" of American democracy remain oblivious to these problems.

The United States deviates from democratic norms. Most established democracies do not use single-member districts to elect their legislators, and those that do generally empower independent commissions to draw the districts. In most nations, a central official or body has responsibility over elections and ensures a minimal level of equality among voters. Voter turnout in most advanced democracies is twenty to thirty points higher than in the United States—in part because many of these nations universally register all eligible citizens rather than shift the responsibility to individuals or interest groups. And, as said in chapter 2, Florida, Kentucky, Virginia, and Armenia are the only democratic systems in the world that ban voting by all former offenders for life.

The initial solutions are simple. Congress should preserve the Voting Rights Act. Federal and state governments should enact checks to prevent partisan abuses of the redistricting process and election administration, as well as meaningful monitoring of election practices. Federal and state governments should also take responsibility for registering all Americans eighteen and older (not unlike the Census Bureau attempts to count all individuals), and should restore voting rights to all former offenders who have completed their sentences. Further, the federal government should fund elections to help enhance equality from one locality to the next.

The aim of this book is not to propose a few piecemeal reforms to patch up democracy, however, but rather to provide a comprehensive approach for examining future problems and reform proposals. An election should be the tool of average citizens rather than of elite political operatives. The vote should allow a meaningful opportunity for citizens to participate in government and check politicians. Voting should also offer "a sense of connectedness to the community and of equal political dignity" and promote broader respect for the legitimacy of society's laws. These benefits are obtained only through access to a fair process—not by a staged process with preset outcomes.[1]

But how do we get there? Elected politicians are unlikely to fall on their swords and pass laws that empower voters. Judges, afraid that they will dirty their hands and lose the appearance of neutrality if they decide political cases, are unlikely to act.

Remaking the matrix of voting is most likely to occur through sustained public pressure by engaged voters and vibrant public interest groups. From the fight for women's suffrage to the struggle for voting rights for Southern blacks in the 1950s and 1960s, engaged citizens have been critical in expanding democracy. In *What Would Jefferson Do?* author Thom Hartmann wrote:

> Systematic change never happens from the top down: it's always from the bottom up. In virtually every case of positive change in the history of democracy, there was each time a groundswell of popular support and a chorus of "average persons' " voices that preceded a nation's leaders taking action.[2]

The problem, however, is that life is overwhelming. Many of us lead busy lives with other important demands. The increased cost of living and the soft economy often require extra time at work, and many people collapse in front of the television when they finally get home. Even the most disciplined people often struggle to exercise and to maintain relationships with family and friends.

Voting requires time—especially in communities with long lines. Working at a polling site on Election Day requires even more time—up to fifteen hours with minimal pay. Accepting responsibility in an organization—whether it is answering phones, calling your state legislator, or testifying before a county election board—requires not only time but sometimes also a sacrifice of other lucrative opportunities.

"I think for me—probably for most people in my age group—people aren't really thinking about civil rights and getting involved actively in civil rights organizations because they are too busy working, trying to make their way, having families, thinking about building wealth," observes Kimberly Perkins, a thirty-year-old litigator who works for the NAACP in Washington, DC. "For the NAACP, where we find our missing component is in the 25–50 age range, and in part it is because they get busy with life and the civil rights struggle of today is not the same civil rights struggle it was when our parents were growing up."

But there are ways to manage the time commitment. "When I

first joined [the League of Women Voters], I was involved in a number of different volunteer things, and I consciously made the decision that I wanted to get deeply involved in one thing rather than dabbling in a number. It was a conscious decision to devote serious time and energy to the League of Women Voters," says Kay Maxwell, who now serves as president (a volunteer, unpaid position) of the nonpartisan organization.

There are also questions about how much good can come from one's sacrifice. The problems with democracy seem so insurmountable that many wonder if their individual involvement will really make a difference. "In this type of activity success doesn't come easily or quickly," explains Jack Taylor, a democracy activist who served as a Roman Catholic priest for twenty-five years before retiring in 1992. "[T]he process of change can be pretty frustrating at times. If someone is going to win in the political process, you have to have a high tolerance for frustration and disgust. . . . I wish it was easier." But there are also rewards. "A bill went through the legislature—that is very fulfilling," Taylor acknowledges. "There is the conviction that you are working on something worthwhile and working with people who share the same kind of convictions—that is very satisfying." Ironically, self-gratification comes from doing something that does not have a direct, immediate return to oneself but benefits the community as a whole. It is the same feeling that motivates a gift on a friend's birthday, a favor for a spouse, or a financial donation to a worthy organization.

The bulk of this book has explained how various parts of the matrix rob voters of choice. But even after one understands the intricacies of the matrix, one might easily ask the question posed by a student after I presented a couple of chapters from this book at my law school over a brown-bag lunch. "Why should we care?" she asked. "Nothing's ever going to change. They won't give up power, and nothing we do—vote, mobilize, protest—is going to change the situation." Others nodded in agreement. I mumbled something about the activism of past generations, but her point stuck with me. Rather than turn toward my school's 500,000-volume library for answers, I decided to ask some of today's activists about the motivations for their involvement.

THE RANCHER

Jack Gould was a busy man. He taught social studies at Raymond Central High just outside of Lincoln, Nebraska; after school, he coached the school football team. Along with his brother, Jack also owned and operated a ranch with 1,800 acres and 600 head of cattle. He and his wife Harriett also had two grade-school–age girls, Donna and Becky.

Despite his obligations, in 1984 Jack accepted an invitation to a meeting of Common Cause, a nonpartisan "good government" group that works to hold politicians accountable through election and government ethics reforms. Jack had been a member since 1973, but he had never been active. Common Cause organizers wanted an average citizen to testify before the state legislature about money in politics, and they offered to help prep the volunteer. Jack signed up. At the time Jack testified, Nebraska had no campaign-finance regulations. The group was successful, and today almost all of Nebraska's state legislative candidates voluntarily agree to limit their spending to $75,000 in order to receive public funds.

Over the years, Jack became increasingly involved and worked on a variety of issues, such as repealing Nebraska's ban on voting by former offenders who completed their sentences. He even served as Common Cause Nebraska's president for two years in the mid-1990s. When its budget was cut in half and several board members resigned, Jack reorganized Common Cause Nebraska into a completely volunteer group.

After twenty-five years of working his ranch, Jack leased out the cattle operation in 2000. At age sixty-two, he runs a B&B with Harriett, which keeps him busy on the weekends. He also volunteers for other organizations, such as the Lincoln Soup Kitchen, where he washes dishes, and he has served as an elder at the Westminster Presbyterian Church. But he remains active in Common Cause and closely monitors legislative issues at the state capital. Jack's two daughters, now twenty-nine and thirty-one, are both members of the organization.

"My participation evolved," Jack explained. "I started out testifying at hearings, then moved to other fields." He admits that he was initially overwhelmed and felt he could never make a dent. But he later learned that "you can pick away. With a good organization and with people who are trying to do the same thing as you are trying to do, you find you can make headway, you can make a difference."

Gumption is an important trait. "It is amazing what happens when you bring something to the floor and there is debate," Jack observes. "You have to bring the issue to them and be willing to stand up. . . . I don't like getting pushed around and I don't like people taking advantage of other people."

When asked about his time commitment, Jack admitted that he doesn't keep track. "I do what has to be done. It's not like a job. It's more like an act of love. You don't just put a time or cost on it." His family's flexibility also helps. "I have a great wife and a brother, who was my partner in the farm work, and they both pick up the slack when I have to go off and crusade. . . . They encourage me to do these things, which makes it very easy."

THE STUDENT

Marcie Graham grew up in Memphis, Tennessee. She went to White Station High, a public school that was about 60 percent white and 40 percent students of color. While most of Marcie's friends were African American, she was one of the few black students in honors classes. She felt different. "There were times when the guidance counselor would give my white counterparts information on things like the SAT IIs," Marcie remembers. "She wouldn't give me the information and I would learn about it through my white friends. You get different experiences where you realize that everything is not equal."

As a teenager, Marcie attended an NAACP youth council meeting because her best friend, Kamilah, had been going. "[O]nce I started going," Marcie said, "I actually got engaged in it." A picket of a local hotel when she was seventeen proved to be a defining event for her. According to court papers, during the Black College Reunion at Daytona Beach in April 1999, the Adam's Mark Hotel forced black guests to purchase and wear a neon-orange identification wristband, fully prepay their hotel bills, and pay deposits of $25 for telephone service, $100 for potential room damage, and $300 for minibar access. These policies did not apply to whites staying at the hotel at the time. The NAACP organized a boycott of all Adam's Mark Hotels, and national NAACP staff who specialized in picketing techniques trained Marcie and other youth council members, local college chapter members, and adult branch members how to avoid being arrested. A group of about fifty showed up in the early morning and remained until the afternoon. Marcie was nervous, but she remained at the site. "It got really intense because there was the possibility that we could be arrested for the picketing that we wanted to do in front of the hotel. That was the first really big mobilization I participated in where you actually got nervous of the consequences of participating."

For Marcie, the experience taught her that "you can have an impact on things" when something is wrong, and that "you're not just going to sit there and not do anything." The Adam's Mark corporation eventually entered into a $1.1 million settlement to resolve legal claims arising from the incident, which included a contribution of $600,000 to four historically black colleges.

At seventeen, Marcie decided to leave the nest and go north for college—to New York University. She was enticed by the school's academic reputation and the fact that it offered her a scholarship. Marcie recalls that there was "definitely a transition," because she didn't have family in Manhattan. Before arriving in the city of eight million, however, she connected with NYU's NAACP chapter, so she immediately had a community. "Because the network is so strong nationally, I knew the regional director who is based in New York from my work with the NAACP in Memphis, so when I came I was able to connect with him instantly. . . . I was able to reach out to [people in NYU's NAACP] and they were supportive of me being here."

Over the next couple of years, Marcie organized several voter-registration and voter-mobilization events on campus. After a summer internship at a record company, she pulled together an "NAACP Voter Registration Jam Down Jumpoff," featuring musical artist Tyrone Houston, a headliner who blends hip-hop and R&B. Houston was the draw, and Marcie set up a table for voter registration and passed out info on absentee voting. More than one hundred students attended, and half of them registered to vote.

Most of Marcie's closest friends are involved with the NAACP. "You recruit by example," Marcie explains. "If everyone sees Marcie, always at the NAACP, people become curious about what is taking up all your time."

"In order to decide whether or not to get involved, the question you need to ask yourself is, what kind of future do you want to have?" Marcie says. "My parents fought so I was able to go to a school that was predominantly white and I was able to get a really good education at a public school, but then you get there and you have to fight to access certain materials. You can be complacent if you want, but you are going to reap the consequences."

Marcie feels that "working with the NAACP makes you feel like you have more of a claim on society" because of the role that one plays in changing it.

THE LAWYER

Odetta MacLeish-White joined the League of Women Voters in 1998—just over a year after she finished her advanced degree in international law at Duke Law School. "I was directed to the League when my boss, my mentor, told me to check it out," Odetta remembers. "It made a lot of sense." The League, which grew out of the women's suffragist movement, is a nonpartisan organization that promotes citizen participation through such activities as voter registration, candidate debates, and election reform.

Odetta's involvement developed gradually. In 2002, the league's Gainesville, Florida, chapter asked her to moderate a "candidate forum"—the league's version of a debate. State representatives, state senators, county commissioners, and school-board officials were up for election that year. Odetta helped develop questions on a broad set of topics and moderated the half-day event. In the following years, Odetta continued to work on candidate forums, soliciting specialized debate questions from different league committees and arranging for local public-radio stations to tape and broadcast the forums.

In 2004, the league's members elected Odetta to the national board at the annual convention, making her, at thirty-four, the youngest person on the national board by eleven years. "I think I bring inexperience, but I also bring a certain amount of youth," she says.

Odetta has grown from her participation. "I was not as politically aware as I have been made by the League, and it has continued to foster my personality and the way I prefer to do things. We look for compromises, and examine things before making judgment calls," she explains. "Before I thought politics had to be partisan. I didn't have a feeling about how I could get in there and participate." Through the league, Odetta has enjoyed many experiences that she would not otherwise have had, such as meeting candidates, participating in conferences, speaking in public, and writing letters-to-the-editor. She also values the social element: "On an extremely personal level, it is a good networking opportunity for me, particularly serving on the national board—meeting women from all over the country. . . . I have met people that I like, and perhaps people who don't get involved don't get that stimulus."

Despite her other obligations, Odetta makes time for the league. She's married to her college sweetheart and works full time for the Florida Housing Finance Corporation as director of the Affordable Housing Study Commission. She also serves on a variety of boards in Gainesville, Florida, including the Chamber of Commerce and Big Brothers/Big Sisters. "You just decide that it's a priority and decide that it's important. I decided that the League had a specific point of view that needed to be told and that point of view is the more wide-ranging, non-partisan approach to politics," Odetta says. When people claim they are too busy to participate, she compares it to the "I'm too busy to exercise thing, which I say to myself on the exercise front all the time, but I know it's a total excuse. . . . I happen to think that my involvement with the League and what we have to offer is extremely important, so I make that time, I make that happen."

THE PASTOR

In about 1996, the Reverend Carrie Bolton had enough. "My parishioners were being laid off after they took their sick children to the doctor a couple of times, there was no day care center, and people injured at a mobile home factory were not being paid their worker's compensation," remembers the fifty-eight-year-old senior pastor at Alston's Chapel United Holy Church, located in the rural town of Pittsboro, North Carolina—population 2,226. Carrie's congregation is predominantly African American, and many are hourly wage line workers in poultry-processing plants, upholstery-fabric plants, and similar places.

"I just felt as though I could not preach the gospel of Jesus Christ on Sunday that talks about abundant life and liberation," she says, "and not work Monday through Saturday to help translate that gospel in a way that impacts the conditions of people. One of the ways to change things was through the ballot box." Carrie worked with other community activists to establish Democracy South, a nonpartisan, multiracial coalition of organizations in the southeastern United States. Democracy South mobilizes around various issues that open doors to working-class and poor people, such as restoring voting rights to former offenders, Election Day voter registration, and campaign-finance reform.

Carrie's mission includes helping members of her flock overcome personal hurdles—such as alcoholism and trouble with the law—but it also extends to reform of elections in North Carolina. "There has to be personal redemption *and* community redemption in order for us to do God's work," Carrie explains. "God calls us to push toward the end that we will feel the need to bring others to redemption and new life." Her work toward this end extends from working with organizations like Democracy South to attending local school-board meetings scheduled "during the day when working folk are unable to attend."

When questioned about the relationship among her faith, democracy, and inequality, Carrie responds:

This is not just about me, myself, and I. This is about us. This is about God's plan for providing for all of God's people. Christ did not talk about survival of the fittest. Jesus talked about how to help the weakest, the most vulnerable, and the poorest rise to their human potential. All the world is God's family. God did not intend for there to be stepchildren.

Individual parishioners occasionally ask Carrie why they should vote or volunteer to change democracy. "You say you are a follower of Christ," Carrie responds. "Christ did not send the earthly ministry into the Temple. Jesus was in the streets. Number one: challenging those who were exploiting the poor. Number two: healing the sick and those who were discouraged. Christ was going against the status quo."

THE STAY-AT-HOME MOM

In 1976, when Nan Morehead's son Ryan started first grade, she realized she would have more free time and wanted to be involved in something larger. Nan called Common Cause Colorado, and soon she was volunteering a couple of days a week in the organization's headquarters. Her initial responsibilities included stuffing envelopes, answering phones, and filing documents. She worked alongside two staffers and a few other volunteers while Ryan was in school, but she always made sure to be home by the time he returned at 3:30 P.M.

"I started out as a stay-at-home mom, who went down to volunteer at an office and stuff envelopes," Nan remembers. "Within a few months, they said, 'We want you to go over to the capital and start following these bills,' so personally, I developed a huge amount of self-confidence and some public-speaking skills. And I did a lot of volunteer lobbying, so certainly developed advocacy and lobbying skills." A year later (in 1977), she was appointed to the board of Common Cause Colorado.

Over the next several years, Nan and others at Common Cause Colorado enjoyed significant victories. "We really have changed the way that legislation was passed in Colorado," Nan said. "Common Cause passed the Sunshine Law in Colorado, so that [government] meetings are open and there is disclosure and accountability." The group also proposed and worked to enact the "Give A Vote to Every Legislator" (GAVEL) ballot initiative, which, Nan says, "ensured that each bill that was introduced had a public hearing and citizens could be a part of it."

Nan has a friend who stayed home washing her patio door every Monday, Wednesday, and Friday morning. "That works for her, but that's clearly not where my priorities were. You let things like that slide," Nan explains. "There were times when I was out collecting signatures rather than washing the windows. . . . If you really care about something, whether it's activism, or playing tennis or bridge, or oil painting—you find the time to make it work."

When Nan's three sons were home from school during vacation periods, they would accompany her to the state capitol building. "They thought it was just a great treat to go to the capitol and climb the 93 steps to the dome. Those were always bribes," she remembers. "You sit here and color and draw pictures while Mommy is in this meeting. Then we'll get to climb to the top of the dome and get to eat in the cafeteria!" The boys would also go with her to festivals and other events. While Nan worked at booths or collected signatures, her sons got their faces painted and checked out the sights. Her husband watched the boys in the evenings when Nan had board meetings.

As they grew into young adults, Nan's sons developed an interest in current events and politics. One of Nan's twin sons, Dan, now thirty years old, remembers going with his mom to the capitol and climbing the stairs to the top of the dome: "She has always been involved in a lot of different awareness groups, and sometimes we'd get toted along to them. It was always an adventure for my brother and me." Dan says that because his mom was always so well informed, "I established my own beliefs and my own thoughts." He indicates that his mother always wanted him "to vote, be active, and have a voice—and I wouldn't have that if it wasn't for her."

In the late 1980s, Nan returned to work full time at the Denver Department of Human Services, where she monitors federal legislation that will have an impact on human services at the city level. Currently, she spends about six to eight hours per month with Common Cause—much less time than in the past. But she has remained active. "To this day, some of my best friends are people I got to know through Common Cause. [Those are bonds] that have really, really stayed there, and that's a huge part of it."

"I have found that it is so true that one person *can* make a difference, and a small group of people can make an even greater difference," Nan states. "If nothing else, we can be consistently well-informed voters—everybody has time for that, and, I think, the obligation to do that."

THE AMERICAN

There had always been much political discussion at the dinner table and within the family circle in Sinaloa, Mexico. But when she was fifteen, Clarissa Martinez De Castro left her hometown and came to the United States with her parents and six siblings. Her family's interest in the political system waned as they grappled with the various challenges imposed by the immigrant experience—a new country, language, and culture. After high school, she studied diplomacy and world affairs at Occidental College in Los Angeles and graduated in 1989.

Today, the thirty-eight-year-old Clarissa serves as the director of state public policy for the National Council of La Raza (NCLR) in Washington, DC. The nonpartisan organization is the leading voice in Washington for improving opportunities for Hispanic Americans, and Clarissa has worked there for ten years. Clarissa's department aims to increase Latino advocacy at the state-government level for people "who do not have a voice as powerful as they should." Specifically, the group helps community-based organizations become conduits of civic engagement for the communities they serve. Clarissa strives to make the organizations more effective agents of change by improving their connection to the electoral process and making them recognized sources of information so that newly eligible voters will turn to them for assistance. Her group provides technical support and helps raise funds for the community-based organizations to help them implement new strategies.

Clarissa was able to "roll up her sleeves" and spend a weekend visiting a mobilization site in Iowa, where Latinos make up merely 2.8 percent of the population but are quickly expanding. Clarissa went to door to door in the Latino community, providing voter information. She remembers hearing from people that "nobody had ever come to their door, that nobody had thought their vote was important. They never got anything in the mail like many other people do, and that was a very important thing for them that somebody had come—that somebody had cared that they should come out and vote."

During the 2004 presidential election, Clarissa and other members of La Raza volunteered to help the National Association of Latino Elected and Appointed Officials (NALEO) with its bilingual hotline when the line became overwhelmed with callers. There had been advertisements for the national hotline, which was a part of the *Ve y Vota* program, on Spanish television and radio; on Election Day, huge numbers of people called to find out where to go to vote and to ask other general questions. "I remember talking to a woman who had gone to three different polling places, but kept insisting until she made it to the right one . . . she had not received the correct information, and by the time she called us and we got back to her, it was very close to closing time," Clarissa explains. After providing the woman with the information she needed, Clarissa did a follow-up phone call and found that the woman did in fact make it to her polling place and was able to vote. "It's incredible. You feel like you are making a big contribution even if it is a small thing."

Through her advocacy, Clarissa found an unexpected benefit— her husband, Douglas, who works for the National Immigration Forum. Though both of their jobs are time-consuming, they still find time for their personal lives. Clarissa now takes art classes to resurrect painting and drawing skills that she has not practiced since college.

While her parents and half of her siblings have returned to Mexico, Clarissa encourages other members of her family to get involved in the voting process. "I have seen relatives that are older and who have been here a long time decide to go through the process even though they were in their fifties or sixties, and that has been very rewarding—and seeing people start talking about politics the way I remember when I was a kid."

Although she has lived in the United States since 1982, Clarissa Martinez De Castro did not become an American citizen until 2001, when she was thirty-four years old. "The immigration process is a complicated process, and the citizenship process can be quite burdensome and a harrowing process at times," she explains. "And once you go through that system—because it is so difficult and because it is so lengthy—you definitely value the fact that going through that process means you are going to be able to vote."

In 2002, Clarissa went to the polls for the first time. "It was exciting, and also a little bit intimidating, just because I had never done it before and did not know exactly what to expect or do—how the machine worked exactly," she remembers. "You realize it's not necessarily an extraordinary occurrence in itself—rather, it's a quiet, no-frills act that nevertheless plays a key role in sustaining and nur-turing democracy and accountability."[3]

While this book details the matrix of election practices that shapes the electorate, at the end of the day American democracy is not just about district lines or politicians. My goal is not to identify a fall guy or single problem that, if addressed, would put democracy on autopilot and relieve us of responsibility. This is really about *us*. It is about whether we continue in our day-to-day lives while others make important decisions for us without any real accountability. It is about whether our kids will have childhood memories of us talk-ing about politics—of parents who seem to exercise some control over their world. It's about whether we will feel detached, alone, and shortchanged—or engaged, empowered, and connected to part of something larger than ourselves. While the matrix of election practices is a web that seemingly allocates power and controls our nation, democracy is a very personal decision—a mindset of resist-ance and independence. The question is whether we will choose to resist the matrix and take control of our lives.

★ ★ ★ ★ ★ ★ ★ ★ ★ ★ ★ ★ ★ ★

ACKNOWLEDGMENTS

Numerous friends, family, and colleagues helped me develop and articulate my thoughts for this book. Their contributions made the book much better than it would have otherwise been, and nothing I write here can fully acknowledge my indebtedness.

A number of people read significant parts of drafts of the book and provided comments that made the text more accurate, readable, and coherent, including: Ian Bassin, Jocelyn Benson, Adam Cox, Jim Drinkard, Heather Gerken, Lani Guinier, Rick Hasen, Grant Hayden, Cynthia Overton, Leslie Overton, Rob Richie, Audrey Steuer, Dan Tokaji, and Fane Wolfer.

Others lent their specialized expertise to help improve particular chapters, including: Angelo Ancheta, Joaquin G. Avila, John Bonifaz, Doug Chapin, Chandler Davidson, Alec Ewald, Margaret Fung, Rodolfo de la Garza, Rosalind Gold, Jon Goldin-Dubois, Jon Greenbaum, Ron Hayduk, Bill Hing, Sam Hirsch, Kevin Johnson, Michael Kang, Daniel Levitas, Glenn Magpantay, Peyton McCrary, Walter Mosley, Michael Pitts, Peter Smith, John Tanner, James Tucker, and Tova Wang.

My thinking was also refined through formal and informal

exchanges with smart people, such as: Ludovic Blain, Barbara Burt, Steve Carbó, Robert Cottrol, Gilda Daniels, Ed Davis, Roger Fairfax, Kathay Feng, Alysia Fischer, Wayne Ford, Kumiki Gibson, Deborah Goldberg, Jonah Goldman, Jehmu Greene, Eddie Hailes, Gerry Hebert, Governor Jim Hodges, Amy Keller, Fred Lawrence, Justin Levitt, Chip Lupu, Marnie Mahoney, Marc Mauer, Lorraine C. Minnite, Susan Molinari, Greg Moore, Steven Mulroy, Ralph Munro, Sean Murphy, Steve Pershing, Nate Persily, Rick Pildes, Judith Reed, Jeffrey Rosen, Michael Selmi, Dinah Shelton, Terry Smith, Karen Stevens, Ron Walters, Michael Waterstone, Wendy Weiser, Catherine Weiss, and Brenda Wright.

I also benefited from various questions and suggestions at talks that I presented about the issues in the book at events organized by the American Constitution Society chapters at Washington and Lee and George Mason University Law Schools, Fair Elections International, George Washington University Law School BLSA, the Lawyers' Committee for Civil Rights, the National Bar Association, and the University of Miami law faculty. My service on the Carter-Baker Commission on Federal Election Reform and the Commission on Presidential Nomination Timing and Scheduling also provided exposure to some important perspectives.

I received substantial support from Deans Fred Lawrence, Roger Trangsrud, and Michael Young at the George Washington University Law School. Librarian Deborah Norwood and Alisa Ridanovic, my assistant, also made my life easier.

On the whole, my research assistants were top notch and vested in this project as though it were their own. Many were more like advisers than assistants and made this a true team effort. Research assistants who worked on this project include Morton Brilliant, DaShondra Brown, Heather Carney, Todd Chatman, Rochelle Claerbaut, Tim Foley, Sharmili Hazra, Brad Hudgins, David Ludwig, Sharese Pryor, Guilherme Roschke, Meredith Sharoky, Dan Taylor, and Cherrie-Ann Walters.

I appreciate the efforts of Michael Bourret at Dystel and Goderich and Amy Cherry and Heather Goodman at W. W. Norton, who were all willing to work with a new author and share with a broad audience the challenges that threaten American democracy.

A book can seem like an overwhelming project, and several people provided various forms of advice, encouragement, and opportunities, including Debo Adegbile, Ryan Alexander, Terry Ao, Nick Bauer, Derek Bok, Julian Bond, Heather Booth, Keith Boykin, Mary Boyle, Donna Brazile, Brandon Briscoe, Paul Butler, Charisse Carney, Sheryll Cashin, Michael Caudell-Feagan, Joi Chaney, Oreese Collins, Jr., Rochelle Collins, Oreese Collins III, Tom Daschle, Angela Davis, Renee DeVigne, Justin Driver, Claire Duggan, Anita Earls, Chris Edley, Chris Elmendorf, Julie Fernandes, Paul Fucito, Karen Gibbs, David Halperin, Cathy Hampton, Alexis Herman, Patricia Jaynes, Robin Jaynes, Kimberly Jenkins, Ted Kalo, Judge Damon J. Keith, Hannibal Kemerer, Randall Kennedy, Orin Kerr, Cynthia Lee, Maryanne Lee, David Lyle, Geri Mannion, Kay Maxwell, Rhonda Medina, Frank Michelman, Martha Minow, Blake Morant, Brandon Neal, Charles Ogletree, Eva Paterson, Ric Patterson, Deval L. Patrick, Chellie Pingree, David Price, Andi Pringle, Miles Rapoport, Steven J. Reyes, Cruz Reynoso, Tim Rusch, Dan Solove, Stephanie Sowell, Michael Strautmanis, Ron Sullivan, Terry Thomas, Elizabeth Warren, Thomasina Williams, Frank Wu, and Raul Yzaguirre. The moral support and prayers of my extended family at the People's Community Baptist Church also allowed for perseverance.

Finally, I thank my wife, Leslie, and my two sons, Sterling and Langston. Family is more important than democracy, and I appreciate the sacrifices they made while I wrote this book.

For more information about this book and the politics of voter suppression, go to www.spenceroverton.com.

APPENDIX

Explanation of Indicators of States' Rankings for Section 5 Coverage

HURDLES

Recent hurdles to voting participation provide a better predictor of future hurdles than obstacles such as literacy tests from 1965. Thus, in chapter 4 the states are ranked according to the number of recent Voting Rights Act objections and claims and the percentage of a state's counties to which the Justice Department sent federal observers.

On a per-county basis, the covered areas with the most Section 5 objections are New York (eight objections for five counties covered), South Carolina (seventy-two objections for forty-six counties covered), and Louisiana (ninety-six objections for sixty-four counties covered). But Section 5 numbers tell only part of the story. The number of Section 2 (which applies nationwide) and Section 203 (bilingual ballots and other language-assistance requirements) cases brought by the Justice Department are also relevant. As a result, I've listed:

1. The fifteen states with the most Section 5 objections filed by the Justice Department and claims brought by the Justice Department under Section 2 and Section 203 of the Voting Rights Act per capita for the ten-year period from January 1995 through December 2004; and
2. The fifteen states that have received the most federal observers per capita between January 1995 and December 2004.

Of course, numbers about recent hurdles may not reveal the whole picture. The numbers of Voting Rights Act objections and claims in Section 5 and Section 203 states may be inflated because they must comply with requirements from which other areas are exempt. This inflation, however, might be offset because the certainty of federal review deters Section 5 states from creating exclusionary election rules, which in turn might reduce the number of Section 2 claims in preclearance states.

ENGAGEMENT

Chapter 4 also ranks states by looking at various factors that are better indicators of the racial health of political markets than whether turnout or registration of all voters in 1964, 1968, or 1972 exceeded 50 percent. Specifically listed are:

1. The fifteen states with the largest gaps between the voting-age citizens of color as a percentage of all citizens and the top-of-the-ticket *statewide elected officials* (including governors, attorneys general, U.S. senators, and secretaries of state) who are people of color and are also the candidate of choice of most minority voters, as a percentage of statewide elected officials of all ethnicities for the ten-year period from January 1995 through December 2004;
2. The fifteen states with the largest gaps between voting-age citizens of color as a percentage of all voters and *all elected officials* of color as a percentage of all elected officials in the ten-year period from January 1995 through December 2004;
3. The fifteen states where the two major-party presidential candidates have been the least competitive with the largest group of minority citizens in the state in the 1996, 2000, and 2004 presidential elections;
4. The fifteen states with the most significant average gap in voter turnout between whites and the largest group of minority citizens in the state in the 1996, 2000, and 2004 presidential elections.
5. The fifteen states with the largest single minority group as a percentage of the total citizen voting-age population; and
6. The fifteen states with the highest percentage of counties covered by Section 203.

There is a significant difference between total number of *all elected officials* in a state and *statewide elected officials*. A state may have a large number of Latino elected officials, for example, because Latinos are segregated in particular districts and are able to elect their candidates of choice. The number of *statewide elected officials* often shows, however, the extent to which whites and voters of color will join together to elect a candidate.

Looking at the extent to which whites are willing to vote for a candidate of color for statewide office and whether both major parties compete for voters of color are rough proxies for the extent to which voters cast ballots along racial lines. As mentioned in chapter 4, we don't have a nationwide assessment of racial bloc voting to precisely compare one area with another because such data usually are collected only for specific localities challenged in Voting Rights Act Section 2 lawsuits. States where one of the major party's presidential candidates repeatedly receives a smaller percentage of the minority vote relative to other states, however, provide some insight. Political candidates and parties that do not compete for voters of color often benefit the most from suppressed voter turnout among people of color.

Some might complain that this approach is unfair because "blacks just aren't Republicans." But such an attitude assumes a fixed, dominant party structure to which voters of color must conform, rather than a system of vibrant parties that evolve to respond to the desires of voters of color and compete for their votes. In some states, for example, the Republican Party is actively reaching out and doing better among black voters than in other states. Healthy political markets encourage political actors to work to win over, rather than exclude, a greater percentage of voters of color.

With regard to the largest disparities in voter turnout between minority and white voting-age citizens in the 1996, 2000, and 2004 presidential elections, turnout might be skewed in swing states. For example, Democrats in the 2004 election might invest heavily in African-American turnout in the swing state of Ohio while ignoring African-American turnout in a solidly red state such as Alabama. While this is a valid concern, the single date and identical candidates of the presidential elections facilitate comparative analysis better than alternatives. For example, comparing turnout among people of color in Democratic gubernatorial primary races across the nation would introduce a diverse set of political issues, candidates, and other variables.

Preclearance coverage is most important in areas that have a large single group of people of color as a percentage of the total citizen voting-age population. In such areas, discrimination may be more rampant because voters of color likely carry more political weight (although this may not be the case in cities and counties that are over 70 percent minority, such as the city of Detroit). For similar reasons, areas with large concentrations of voters who require language assistance are relevant. Section 203 requires language assistance in jurisdictions in which more than 5 percent of the voting-age citizens (or more than 10,000 voting-age citizens) belong to a single-language minority community and have limited English proficiency, and the illiteracy rate of the language minority citizens is higher than the national illiteracy rate. The statute's coverage formula reflects concentrations of language minorities.

CONCERNS WITH FACTORS

My analysis focuses on states, and one could argue that only the most problematic counties or cities within a state should be covered by Section 5.

Readers interested in a particular locality should apply these factors to examine localities.

Also, officials in a state such as Louisiana might argue that candidates of color in their state have simply not possessed the qualifications to attract more discerning white voters. They might also note that racial disparities in elected officials are much less severe than in 1965. But my analysis does not use 1965 or the status of Louisiana whites as the ultimate comparative baseline, but rather data from racial disparities in other states. Thus, if racial gaps in elected officials are much smaller in Louisiana than in the uncovered state of Minnesota, why should we continue Section 5 coverage in Louisiana while Minnesota remains exempt? But if the racial gaps in Louisiana are larger, why should Congress suspend Section 5 coverage in Louisiana? Having established the effectiveness of Section 5, the final issue is to determine the proper ordering of states so that we focus our enforcement resources on the most racially exclusionary areas.

Some will claim that states covered by Section 5 have a built-in bias because the law requires investigations for preclearance purposes and forces the Department of Justice to search for problems. That is true to some extent, but the concern is mitigated by the fact that several states with full or significant Section 5 coverage—such as Virginia, Alaska, Georgia, North Carolina, and Texas—did not prompt the investigations per capita prompted by Mississippi, Arizona, and Alabama. Further, Illinois, Indiana, New Jersey, New Mexico, Pennsylvania, and Utah, which are currently not covered by Section 5, also appear on the list.

That said, a few will argue that some of the metrics I have listed do not indicate unhealthy political markets. No set of factors will please all. Thus, I have isolated and discussed each item separately so that readers can discount any variables they believe are less relevant. The most important matter is to put the factors on the table for debate.

Also, chapter 4 does not balance or weigh the factors. If a state falls in the top 30 percent of states in a particular factor (my reason for choosing the "top fifteen states"), then the state joins the list. (I do list the states from most to least extreme within the top 30 percent.) Any attempt to quantify numerically the differences among the top 30 percent of states would become excessively complex without adding a great deal of information.

DISCLAIMER

Some civil-rights advocates might be nervous about discussing whether the coverage formula is tailored to require preclearance of the most troubling areas, fearful that the exercise opens a Pandora's box that leads toward the death of Section 5. Once we start to evaluate the coverage formula, the argument goes, politicians who receive few minority votes will jockey to manipulate the test to avoid coverage of their state—not unlike the way politicians maneuver to keep open their states' obsolete U.S. military bases.

I am sensitive to these concerns. Even though Section 5's effectiveness as a legal tool is entirely separate from whether the coverage formula should be revised, I understand that some may attack the coverage formula as a strategy to eliminate Section 5. On the other hand, a U.S. Supreme Court focused on federalism might question whether a 1960s coverage formula most accurately targets voting problems in the twenty-first century. Certainly, Congress should examine contemporary voting problems in states covered by any renewed coverage formula. At the same time, however, by developing factors of racial dysfunction—and examining states relative to one another with the metric—Congress can ensure the effectiveness of any coverage formula it adopts.

★ ★ ★ ★ ★ ★ ★ ★ ★ ★ ★ ★ ★ ★

NOTES

Introduction

1. See Samuel Issacharoff, Pamela S. Karlan, Richard H. Pildes, *The Law of Democracy: Legal Structure of the Political Process* (New York: Foundation, 1998).

2. Josh Burek, "The Gospel According to Neo," *Christian Science Monitor*, May 9, 2003, available at www.csmonitor.com/2003/0509/p16s01-almo.html; Stephanie Schorow, "Caught in 'The Matrix'—Reality Is, Filmgoers Show True Love for Surprising Hit by Watching it Again and Again," *Boston Herald*, August 2, 1999; Richard Natale, "Through the Looking Glass," *Los Angeles Times*, October 30, 2000; Bob Strauss, "Mind Over 'Matrix': Wachowskis' Goal: Make High-Tech Action Film a Quantum Leap Above the Dumbed-Down Genre," *Daily News of Los Angeles*, March 31, 1999; Issacharoff, Karlan, and Pildes, *The Law of Democracy*.

Chapter One

1. In the fourteen other states, districting maps are drawn by commissions.

2. Miguel Bustillo and Nicholas Riccardi, "Census 2000: Lining Up to Redraw the Political Map," *Los Angeles Times*, March 31, 2001; Common Cause, "Designer Districts," www.commoncause.org/atf/cf/{FB3C17E2-CDD1-4DF6-92BE-BD4429893665}/CCDesignerDisricts_FINAL_2.pdf (accessed May 24, 2005); Editorial, "Serving the Pols, Not the People," *Los Angeles Times*, November 10, 2004; Thomas B. Edsall, "A Political Fight to Define the Future; Latinos at Odds Over California's Two New

Democratic Congressional Districts," *Washington Post*, October 31, 2001; Steve Geissinger, "Competitive Races Exist Only on Fringe of Bay Area," *San Mateo County Times*, October 19, 2002; Timm Herdt, "Landscape of Redrawn Districts Gives Many a Free Ride," *Ventura County Star*, October 7, 2001; Hanh Quach and Dena Bunis, "All Bow to Redistrict Architect: Politics Secretive, Single-minded Michael Berman Holds All the Crucial Cards," *Orange County Register*, August 26, 2001; Howard Kurtz, "California Losers Staked All on Hardball Media Ads," *Washington Post*, June 7, 1992; Alan Miller, "Mr. Inside & Mr. Outside: The Audacious Berman Brothers Built a Powerful Progressive Machine in California. But Can They Survive a New Political Order?" *Los Angeles Times,* March 29, 1992; Jay Mathews, "California Redistricting Heats Up; Ballot Initiatives Spark Sharp Fight," *Washington Post*, June 1, 1990; Carl Ingram, "Plan to Redraw Districts Passes," *Los Angeles Times*, September 14, 2001; Carl Ingram and Jean Merl, "Safe Seats Mean Few Voters Get Real Choice," *Los Angeles Times*, October 27, 2002; Putnam "Put" Livermore, "Political Power Lines," *San Diego Union-Tribune*, July 1, 2001; John Marelius, "Battle Lines Are Drawn as Redistricting Begins," *San Diego Union-Tribune*, May 21, 2001; John Marelius, "Legislative Redistricting in Reform Plan," Copley News Service, January 23, 2005, www.lexisnexis.com/; Lisa Plendl, "No Room for Voters," State Net 32, no. 1 (2002): 12, www.lexisnexis.com/; Kenneth Reich, "Latino Group Sues Over Redistricting," *Los Angeles Times*, October 2, 2001; Jim Sanders, "Democrats Still Rule Legislature, but . . . ," *Sacramento Bee*, November 7, 2002; Elections Division, California Secretary of State, "Statement of Vote—2002 General Election," www.ss.ca.gov/elections/sov/2002_general/contents.htm (accessed June 9, 2005); "Legislature Convenes," Copley News Service, December 6, 2004, www.lexisnexis.com/.

3. Samuel Hirsch, "The United States House of Unrepresentatives: What Went Wrong in the Latest Round of Congressional Redistricting," *Election Law Journal* 2 (2003): 179, 206–207; Joseph C. Coates III, "The Court Confonts the Gerrymander," 15 Fla. St. U.L. Rev. 351, 352 n.11; *Vieth v. Jubelirer,* 124 S. Ct. 1769, 1774 (2004); Hirsch, "The United States House of Unrepresentatives": 184–87; Common Cause, "Redistricting," www.commoncause.org/site/pp.asp?c=dkLNK1MQIw G&b=196481 (accessed June 9, 2005); The Center for Voting and Democracy, "Dubious Democracy: Texas," at www.fairvote.org/dubdem/tx.htm (accessed July 28, 2005); Elections Division, Texas Secretary of State, 2004 General Election, available at http://elections.sos.state.tx.us/elchist.exe (accessed June 9, 2005); Samuel Issacharoff and Richard H. Pildes, "Politics as Markets: Partisan Lockups of the Democratic Process,"

Stanford Law Review 50 (1998): 708–9; Nathaniel Persily, "In Defense of Foxes Guarding Henhouses: The Case for Judicial Acquiescence to Incumbent-Protecting Gerrymanders," *Harvard Law Review* 116 (2002): 649, 672; Samuel Issacharoff, "Why Elections?" *Harvard Law Review* 116 (2002): 684, 687; Nathaniel Persily, "Candidates v. Parties: The Constitutional Constraints on Primary Ballot Access Laws," *Georgetown Law Journal* 89 (2001): 2181, 2190; Samuel Issacharoff and Richard H. Pildes, "Politics as Markets: 646; Samuel Issacharoff, "Gerrymandering and Political Cartels," *Harvard Law Review* 116 (2002): 593, 600, 615; *The Federalist, No. 51*: 349 (James Madison) (Jacob E. Cooke, ed., 1961); Don Herzog, *Happy Slaves: A Critique of Consent Theory* (Chicago: University of Chicago Press, 1989), 205–7; Hanna Fenichel Pitkin, *The Concept of Representation* (Berkeley: University of California Press, 1967), 232; Samuel Issacharoff, "Why Elections?": 684; Michael J. Klarman, "Majoritarian Judicial Review: The Entrenchment Problem," *Georgetown Law Journal* 85 (1997): 491, 498 ; Richard H. Pildes, "The Theory of Political Competition," *Virginia Law Review* 85 (1999): 1605, 1611; Ronald Dworkin, *Life's Dominion* (New York: Knopf, 1993), 222; Cass R. Sunstein, *Democracy and the Problem of Free Speech* (New York: Free Press, 1995), 138; Erwin Chemerinsky, "The Supreme Court, 1988 Term: Foreword: The Vanishing Constitution," *Harvard Law Review* 103 (1989): 75; Michael H. Shapiro, "Judicial Selection and the Design of Clumsy Institutions," *Southern California Law Review* 61 (1988): 1555, 1567 n. 48; Joseph Raz, *The Morality of Freedom* (Oxford: Oxford University Press, 1986), 373–77.

4. Brian E. Crowley, "Elections Chief Rejects Recount: Counting on Hold as Courts Wrangle," *Palm Beach Post,* November 16, 2000; Michael Cooper, "Counting the Vote: The Secretary of State," *New York Times,* November 14, 2000; Jeffrey Toobin, *Too Close to Call: The Thirty-Six-Day Battle to Decide the 2000 Election* (New York: Random House, 2002), 62; Abner Green, *Understanding the 2000 Election: A Guide to the Legal Battles That Decided the Presidency* (New York: New York University Press, 2001), 45–61; Nancy Dunne, "Desperate Observers Monitor the Counters," *Financial Times*, November 21, 2000; Monica Davey, "Court Blocks Certification of Votes; Hero or Hack, Harris on the Hot Seat," *Chicago Tribune*, November 18, 2000; Richard L. Hasen, "Beyond the Margin of Litigation: Reforming U.S. Election Administration to Avoid Electoral Meltdown," *Washington and Lee Law Review* 62 (2005); Kristin L. Adair, "Keeping Up Appearances: The Role of Partisan Politics in U.S. Election Administration and the Need for Reform" (unpublished manuscript, 2005); Einer Elhauge, "Florida 2000: Bush Wins Again!" *Weekly*

Standard, November 26, 2001, 29; "An Umpire Taking Sides," *New York Times*, July 9, 2004; Tim Reiterman, "Secretary of State Shelley Steps Down," *Los Angeles Times*, February 5, 2005; William March, "Harris' Vote Certification Deadline Criticized," *Tampa Tribune*, November 14, 2000; Keith Epstein, "Partisan Hands Run Election Process," Media General News Service, October 4, 2004, http://washdateline. mgnetwork.com/index.cfm?SiteID=wsh&PackageID=46&fuseaction=arti cle.main&ArticleID=6222&GroupID=214; Keith Ervin and David Postman, "County Discovers 87 More Untallied Ballots," *Seattle Times*, April 2, 2005; Kenneth P. Vogel, "Sam Reed: Behind the Sound Bite," *Tacoma* [WA] *News Tribune*, January 1, 2005; David Postman, "Republican Reed Faces GOP Wrath over Recount Decisions," *Seattle Times*, January 3, 2005; Thomas Shapley, "This Is no Time to Be Slow Dancing on Voting Reform," *Seattle Post-Intelligencer*, January 16, 2005, http://seattlepi.nwsource.com/opinion/207913_capit0116.html; Zachary Coile, "Election Chief Tries to Allay Fears," *San Francisco Chronicle*, May 6, 2005, A19; Esther Schrader and Tim Reiterman, "Audit Adds to Troubles for Shelley," *Los Angeles Times*, January 28, 2005, B6; Hasen, "Beyond the Margin of Litigation"; Rafael Lopez-Pintor, *Electoral Management Bodies as Institutions of Governance* (New York: United National Development Programme, 2000).

5. Transcript of Gettysburg Address (1863), www.ourdocuments.gov/ doc.php?flash=true&doc=36&page=transcript; Gaetano Mosca, "The Ruling Class," in *Princeton Readings in Political Thought* (Princeton, NJ: Princeton University Press, 1996), 512; Richard A. Posner, *Law, Pragmatism, and Democracy* (Cambridge: Harvard University Press, 2003), 130; Joseph Schumpeter, *Capitalism, Socialism and Democracy* (New York: Harper and Row, 1975); John F. Burns and James Glanz, "Iraqi Shiites Win, but Margin Is Less than Projection," *New York Times*, February 14, 2005; Fair Vote—Political Empowerment Program, "Cumulative Voting: A Commonly Used Full Representation Method," www.fairvote.org/cumulative/.

6. "2004 U.S. Election: An International Perspective," Fair Election International, November 5, 2004, www.fairelection.us/fairelectionre port.pdf; Christopher S. Elmendorf, "Representation Reinforcement Through Advisory Commissions: The Case of Election Law," *New York University Law Review* 80 (2005); David Butler and Bruce E. Cain, *Congressional Redistricting: Comparative and Theoretical Perspectives* (New Jersey: Prentice Hall, 1992), 117–28; John C. Courtney, "Redistricting: What the United States Can Learn from Canada," *Election*

Law Journal 3 (2004): 499; Persily, "Reply: In Defense of Foxes Guarding Henhouses": 649, 674.

7. Hasen, "Beyond the Margin of Litigation"; National Association of Secretaries of State, "Administering Elections in a Nonpartisan Manner," news release, February 6, 2005, www.nass.org/electioninfo/Statement% 20on%20Partisanship%20Issue.pdf (accessed June 9, 2005); Frederick Schauer, "Judicial Review of the Devices of Democracy," *Columbia Law Review* 94 (1994): 1326.

8. See Jeffrey Rosen, *Divided Suffrage*, 12 CONST. COMM. 199, 200–1 (1995); Elmendorf, "Representation Reinforcement Through Advisory Commissions"; Heather K. Gerken, "The Double-Edged Sword of Independence: Inoculating Electoral Reform Commissions Against Everyday Politics" (in progress, 2005); Leo Perra, A Presentation on Province-Wide Citizen Participation (July 13, 2004), available at www.citizensassembly.bc.ca/ resources/china/China_presentation.pdf (accessed July 26, 2005).

Chapter Two

1. Michael Powell and Peter Slevin, "Several Factors Contributed to 'Lost' Voters in Ohio," *Washington Post*, December 15, 2004; Geoff Dutton, "Suburbs Were Busiest, Even with More Machines," *Columbus Dispatch*, November 5, 2004; Election Process Information Collection, "EPIC Comparative Analysis: Electoral Management," http://epicproject.org/ace/ compepic/en/EM02 (accessed July 10, 2005); Dorothy Turner, interview by Dan Taylor, July 10, 2005; Sharon Priest, "The Secretaries Speak: Sixteen Points to Improve American Elections," *Election Law Journal* 1 (2002): 71; Alec Ewald, "American Voting: The Local Character of Suffrage in the United States" (unpublished dissertation, February 2005), 2; Jimmy Carter et al., *To Assure Pride and Confidence in the Electoral Process: Report of the National Commission on Federal Election Reform* (2002), 27; Office of the Secretary of State, State of Alabama, "County Election Officials Inquiry," www.sos.state.al.us/cf/election/borjop1.cfm (accessed July 10, 2005); U.S. Election Assistance Commission, "The Administrative Structure of State Election Offices," www.eac.gov/elec tion_resources/tech3.htm, (accessed July 10, 2005); Bengt Säve-Söderbergh, Institute for Democracy and Electoral Assistance, "Broader Lessons of the U.S. Election Drama," www.idea.int/press/op_ed_08.htm; Elections Canada, "Compendium of Election Administration in Canada: A Comparative Overview" (2003): 17–31, www.elections.ca/loi/com2003/ compoverview2003_e.pdf (accessed July 10, 2005); James L. Robertson,

Library of Parliament, "The Canadian Electoral System," www.parl.gc.ca/-information/library/PRBpubs/bp437-e.htm (2004) (accessed July 10, 2005).

2. Fritz Wenzel, "Purging of Rolls, Confusion Anger Voters," *Toledo Blade*, January 9, 2005, toledoblade.com/apps/pbcs.dll/article?AID=/20050109/ NEWS09/501090334 (accessed June 25, 2005); National Conference of State Legislatures, "Voter Registration Deadlines," www.ncsl.org/pro grams/legman/elect/taskfc/deadlines.htm (accessed July 10, 2005); Daniel P. Tokaji, "How Did Ohio's Voting Equipment Fare in 2004?" http://morit zlaw.osu.edu/electionlaw/comments/2005/comment0208.html (accessed July 10, 2005); Daniel P. Tokaji, "The Paperless Chase: Electronic Voting and Democratic Values," *Fordham Law Review* 73 (2005): 1737; The Sentencing Project, "Felony Disenfranchisement Laws in the United States," www.sentencingproject.org/pdfs/1046.pdf (accessed July 13, 2005); Jeremy Travis, "Invisible Punishment: An Instrument of Social Exclusion," in *Invisible Punishment*, ed. Marc Mauer and Meda Chesney-Lind (New York:New Press, 2003).

3. U.S. Constitution, art. 1, sec. 4, cl. 1; U.S. Constitution, art. 4, sec. 4; U.S. Constitution, art. 1, sec. 8, cl. 1; *Voting Rights Act, U.S. Code* 42, sec. 1971; *Voting Accessibility for the Elderly and Handicapped Act, U.S. Code* 42, sec. 1973ee; *The Uniformed and Overseas Citizens Absentee Voting Act, U.S. Code* 42, sec. 1973ff; *National Voter Registration Act, U.S. Code* 42, sec. 1973gg; *Help America Vote Act, U.S. Code* 42, sections 15301–15545; *Oregon v. Mitchell*, 400 U.S. 112 (1970).

4. National Association of Secretaries of State to Members of Congress (February 6, 2005), www.nass.org/Open%20Letter%20to%20Congress2.pdf (accessed June 24, 2005); John Samples, "Election Reform, Federalism, and the Obligations of the Voters," *Policy Analysis* 417 (2001), www.cato.org/pubs/pas/pa417.pdf (accessed June 24, 2005); Akhil Reed Amar, "Five Views of Federalism: 'Converse-1983' in Context," *Vanderbilt Law Review* 47 (1994): 1229; Heather K. Gerken, "Second-Order Diversity," *Harvard Law Review* 118 (2005): 1099; Dennis Thompson, *Just Elections*, chap. 3, "Popular Sovereignty: Who Decides What Votes Count" (Chicago: University of Chicago Press, 2002), 180; Alec C. Ewald, "American Voting: The Local Character of Suffrage in the United States" (unpublished dissertation, February 2005); Jennifer Hochschild, "Introduction and Comments," 1 *Perspectives on Politics* 247 (2003), 247–48.

5. FairVote, "Vote by Mail," at www.fairvote.org/turnout/mail.htm (accessed August 1, 2005); Oregon Secretary of State Bill Bradbury, Remarks to the Public Forum on Election Integrity (February 18, 2005), available at

www.sos.state.or.us/executive/speeches/021805.htm (accessed August 1, 2005); *Federal Energy Regulatory Commission v. Mississippi*, 456 U.S. 742, 788–91 (1982) (O'Connor, J., concurring in the judgment in part and dissenting in part); Amar, "Five Views of Federalism": 1229; Ewald, "American Voting"; Ronald Hayduk, *Democracy for All: Restoring Immigrant Voting in the United States* (London: Routledge, 2005); Joel Engelhardt and Scott McCabe, "Over-votes Cost Gore the Election in FL," *Palm Beach Post*, March 11, 2001, available at http://65.40.245.240/-voxpop/palmpost.htm.

6. Election Process Information Collection, "EPIC Comparative Analysis: Electoral Management," http://epicproject.org/ace/compepic/en/coun try$ZW+EM (last accessed July 10, 2005); Michael Wines, "Zimbabwe Opposition Promises to Spell Out Election Fraud," *New York Times*, April 6, 2005; Priest, "The Secretaries Speak": 71; *The Federalist, No. 51* (James Madison); Alexis de Tocqueville, *Democracy in America, Vol. I* (1835), (New York: Vintage, 1990), 71, 404; Amar, "Five Views of Federalism": 1229; Michael W. McConnell, "Federalism: Evaluating the Founders' Design," *University of Chicago Law Review* 54 (1987): 1484; Dahleen Glanton, "Restoring Felons' Voting Rights a Heated Election-Year Issue in Fla.," *Chicago Tribune*, July 28, 2004; Shawn Macomber, "Re-Enfranchising Felons," *American Spectator*, March 2, 2005; Kevin Krajick, "Why Can't Ex-Felons Vote?" *Washington Post*, August 18, 2004, A19; The Sentencing Project, "Felony Disenfranchisement Laws in the United States"; Christopher Uggen and Jeff Manza, "Democratic Contraction? Political Consequences of Felon Disenfranchisement in the United States," American Sociological Review 67 (2002): 777, 786, 788, 793; Brandon Rottinghaus, "Incarceration and Enfranchisement: International Practices, Impact, and Recommendations for Reform," International Foundation for Election Systems, Washington, DC, June–July 2003, www.sentencingpro-ject.org/pdfs/Rottinghaus.pdf (accessed May 29, 2005); Angela Behrens, Christopher Uggen, and Jeff Manza, "Ballot Manipulation and the 'Menace of Negro Domination': Racial Threat and Felon Disenfranchisement in the United States, 1850–2002," American Journal of Sociology 109 (2003): 562; Uggen and Manza, "Democratic Contraction?" 798.

7. Richard Briffault, "Our Localism: Part II—Localism and Legal Theory," *Columbia Law Review* 90 (1990): 346; David J. Barron, "A Localist Critique of the New Federalism," *Duke Law Journal* 51 (2001): 377; Gerken, "Second-Order Diversity": 1099; Amar, "Five Views of Federalism": 1229; CalTech/MIT Voting Technology Project, "Voting: What Is, What Could Be" (2001), 50; Office of Management and Budget,

The White House, "Budget of the United States Government, FY 2006," available at www.whitehouse.gov/omb/budget/fy2006/defense.html (accessed July 28, 2005).

Chapter Three

1. John Hill, " 'It's a Tossup,' " *Daily Town Talk* (Alexandria, LA), December 5, 2002, 1A; "Fields Drops Senate Bid," *The Advocate* (Baton Rouge, LA), August 8, 2002, 10B; Katharine Q. Seelye, "In Louisiana, a Democrat Wins a Tough Senate Race," *New York Times*, December 8, 2002, sec. 1, 37; Lee Hockstader and Adam Nossiter, "GOP Outmaneuvered in La. Runoff," *Washington Post*, December 9, 2002, A4; "Veteran Political Observers Say Sugar Imports, Steel Tariffs, Late Effort by Bill Clinton Help Landrieu Hold LA Senate Seat," *White House Bulletin*, December 9, 2002; Lev Grossman, "One More for the Dems," *Time*, December 16, 2002: 19.

2. U.S. Census Bureau, "USA Quickfacts," http://quickfacts.census.gov/qfd/states/00000.html; Jennifer Cheeseman Day and Kelly Holder, "Voting and Registration in the Election of November 2002," *Current Population Reports*, July 2004, www.census.gov/prod/2004pubs/p20-552.pdf, 5; Ethnic Majority, "African, Hispanic (Latino), and Asian American Members of Congress," www.ethnicmajority.com/congress.htm; Guy-Uriel E. Charles, "Racial Identity, Electoral Structures, and the First Amendment Right of Association," *California Law Review* 91 (2003): 1209 (www.umich.edu/~nes/nesguide/nesguide.htm; http://webapp .icpsr.umich.edu/cocoon/ICPSR-SERIES/00163.xml; and also Pew); Paul Duggan, "Houston Reelects Mayor in Close Race," *Washington Post*, December 3, 2001, A2; Lori Rodriguez, "Sanchez Scores Win for Latinos," *Houston Chronicle*, December 9, 2001, A1; Greg J. Borowski, "Pratt Boosted Black Turnout," *Milwaukee Journal-Sentinel*, April 8, 2004, 17A; Larry Sandler and Leonard Sykes, Jr., "A Race in Which Race Didn't Matter," *Milwaukee Journal-Sentinel*, November 4, 2004, B1; Michael C. Dawson, *Behind the Mule: Race and Class in African-American Politics* (Princeton, NJ: Princeton University Press, 1994), 115–16; Katherine Tate, *From Protest to Politics: The New Black Voters in American Elections* (Cambridge: Harvard University Press, 1993), 40–42; Charles, "Racial Identity, Electoral Structures, and the First Amendment Right of Association": 1236; Donald R. Kinder and Lynn M. Sanders, *Divided by Color: Racial Politics and Democratic Ideals* (Chicago: University of Chicago Press, 1996), 33; Bernard Grofman et al., "Drawing Effective Minority Districts: A Conceptual Framework and Some Empirical Evidence," *North Carolina Law Review* 79 (2001): 1401 (of the 17 pre-

dominantly minority districts studied, only one black candidate, Bobby Scott from Virginia, received a majority of white votes); Charles S. Bullock III and Richard E. Dunn, "The Demise of Racial Districting and the Future of Black Representation," *Emory Law Journal* 48 (1999): 1250; Grofman et al., "Drawing Effective Minority Districts": 1402; Michael Kranish and Brian McGrory, "Democrats Show Spunk, Blunting Republican Gains," *Boston Globe*, November 4, 1998, A1 ("[Democratic] officials said last night that the party spent three times as much money on voter turnout this year compared with the last two elections, with a special emphasis on black and Hispanic voters."); Stewart M. Powell and Mark Helm, "Parties Gear Up Quest to Win Hispanic Votes," *San Antonio Express-News*, November 8, 1998, A17. Compare also www.cnn.com/ELECTION/1998/states/NV/S/exit.poll.html with www.cnn.com/ELECTION/1998/states/NV/polls/NV96PH.html (showing Hispanic voters composed 5 percent of the 1998 Nevada turnout vs. 3 percent in 1996); U.S. Bureau of Census, Washington, DC, Annual Estimates of the Population by Race Alone or in Combination and Hispanic or Latino Origin for the United States and States: July 1, 2003; www.cnn.com/ELECTION/2004/pages/results/states/WA/G/00/epolls.0.html; Jonathan Nagler and R. Michael Alvarez, "Latinos, Anglos, Voters, Candidates and Voting Rights," *University of Pennsylvania Law Review* 153 (2004): 393; Richard Skinner and Philip A. Klinkner, "Black, White, Brown and Cajun: The Racial Dynamics of the 2003 Louisiana Gubernatorial Election," *The Forum* 2 (2004): 1–2; Steve Schultze and Greg J. Borowski, "Barrett defeats Pratt 54%–46%," *Milwaukee Journal-Sentinel*, April 7, 2004; Adam Nossiter, "Study Suggests Bias, Ex-Duke Voters Defeated Jindal," Associated Press, April 9, 2004; Adam Nossiter, "Did Racism Beat Jindal?" Associated Press, December 5, 2003.

3. *Rogers v. Lodge*, 458 U.S. 613, 651 (1982) (Stevens, J., dissenting). See also *Mobile v. Bolden*, 446 U.S. 55, 87–88 (1980) (Stevens, J., concurring); *Karcher v. Daggett*, 462 U.S. 725, 748 (1983) (Stevens, J., concurring opinion); *Vieth v. Jubelirer*, 541 U.S. 267, 327 (2004) (Stevens, J., dissenting); *Cousins v. City Council of Chicago*, 466 F.2d 830, 850–853 (CA7 1972) (Stevens, J., dissenting); Pamela S. Karlan, "Cousins' Kin: Justice Stevens and Voting Rights," *Rutgers Law Journal* 27 (1996): 521.

4. Lazos Vargas, "Deconstructing Homo[geneous] Americanus": 1577.

5. Dixon Ryan Fox, "The Negro Vote in Old New York," *Political Science Quarterly* 2 (June 1917): 252–75; Robert Cottrol, *The Afro-Yankees: Providence's Black Community in the Antebellum Era* (Westport, CT: Greenwood Press, 1982).

6. Pew Hispanic Center, "The Wealth of Hispanic Households: 1996 to 2002" (2004); Bureau of Justice Statistics, "Prison and Jail Inmates at Year 2001," www.prisonpolicy.org/graphs/US_incrates2001.shtml; http://print .infoplease.com/ipa/A0774057.html; U.S. Bureau of the Census, *We the People: Asians in the United States* (2004), 11; U.S. Bureau of the Census, *We the People: Hispanics in the United States* (2004), 10.

7. Sylvia R. Lazos Vargas, "The Latina/o and APIA Vote Post-2000: What Does It Mean to Move Beyond 'Black and White' Politics?" *Oregon Law Review* 81 (2002): 794–95, 798–99; Lazos Vargas, "Deconstructing Homo [geneous] Americanus": 1501; U.S. Bureau of the Census, *Population Projections of the United States by Age, Sex, Race and Hispanic Origin: 1995 to 2050* (1996); Kevin Johnson, "Latinas/os and the Political Process: The Need for Critical Inquiry," *Oregon Law Review* 81 (2002): 917; U.S. Immigration and Naturalization Service, *Annual Report: Legal Immigration, Fiscal Year 2001* (2002), 2.

8. Lani Guinier and Gerald Torres, *The Miner's Canary: Enlisting Race, Resisting Power, Transforming Democracy* (Cambridge: Harvard University Press, 2002).

9. See Richard Hasen, "Vote Buying," *California Law Review* 88 (2000): 1356 n.175.

Chapter Four

1. Confederate States of America, "Declaration of the Immediate Causes Which Induce and Justify the Secession of South Carolina from the Federal Union," December 24, 1860, www.yale.edu/lawweb/avalon/csa/ scarsec.htm; Selwyn Carter, "African American Voting Rights: An Historical Struggle," *Emory Law Journal* 44 (1995): 859; Maurine Christopher, *America's Black Congressmen* (New York: Crowell, 1971), 164; Manning Marable, "Stealing the Election: The Compromises of 1876 and 2000," *Standards* 7, no. 2 (2001), www.colorado.edu/journals/stan-dards/V7N2/FIRST/marable.html; ACLU, "Reaffirmation or Requiem for the Voting Rights Act? The Court Will Decide." (May 1995) http://archive. aclu.org/issues/racial/racevote.html; Samuel Issacharoff, Pamela S. Karlan, Richard H. Pildes, *The Law of Democracy: Legal Structure of the Political Process*, 2d rev. ed. (New York: Foundation, 2002), 90; Morgan Kousser, *The Shaping of Southern Politics: Suffrage Restrictions and the Establishment of the One-Party South, 1880–1910* (New Haven, CT: Yale University Press, 1974), 63–72; Blanche Bong Cook, "A Paradigm for Equality: The Honorable Damon J. Keith," *Wayne Law Review* 47 (2002): 1161; Barry E. Hawk and John J. Kirby, Jr., "Federal Protection of Negro

Voting Rights," *Virginia Law Review* 51, no. 6 (October 1965): 1093–96; Issacharoff, Karlan, and Pildes, *The Law of Democracy*: 117–24; 546–47; John Lewis, *Walking with the Wind: A Memoir of the Movement* (New York: Harcourt Brace, 1998), 300–62; C. Vann Woodward, *The Strange Career of Jim Crow* (New York: Oxford University Press, 1955).

2. Bernard Grofman et al., *Minority Representation and the Quest for Voting Equality* (New York: Cambridge University Press, 1992), 22; Edward Blum and Roger Clegg, "Color Inside the Lines," *Legal Affairs*, 2003; Samuel Issacharoff and Pamela S. Karlan, "Groups, Politics, and the Equal Protection Clause," *University of Miami Law Review* 58 (2003): 35; ACLU, "Reaffirmation or Requiem for the Voting Rights Act?"; Rodolfo O. de la Garza and Louis DeSipio, "Save the Baby, Change the Bathwater, and Scrub the Tub: Latino Electoral Participation after Seventeen Years of Voting Rights Act Coverage," *Texas Law Review* 71 (1993): 1495.

3. *Allen v. State Bd. of Elections*, 393 U.S. 544 (1969).

4. Grofman et al., *Minority Representation and the Quest for Voting Equality*, 22; Blum and Clegg, "Color Inside the Lines"; Issacharoff and Karlan, "Groups, Politics, and the Equal Protection Clause": 35; ACLU, "Reaffirmation or Requiem for the Voting Rights Act?"; de la Garza and DeSipio, "Save the Baby, Change the Bathwater": 1495.

5. Jon Greenbaum, e-mail message to author, March 15, 2005; Terry Kliewer, "Letter by Waller County DA Spurs Criticism from Blacks," *Houston Chronicle*, December 10, 2003; *United States v. Texas*, 445 F. Supp. 1245, 1250–52 (1978); Rebecca McPhail, "Prairie View Students May Escape Jail Terms," *Daily Cougar* (University of Houston, TX), April 16, 1992; Terry Kliewer, "Waller County Officials Say Race, Politics Behind Probes," *Houston Chronicle*, August 5, 2003; Terry Kliewer, "Charge Dropped Against Former Justice of Peace," *Houston Chronicle*, August 8, 2003; Terry Kliewer, "Feds to Investigate Prairie View Flap," *Houston Chronicle*, January 23, 2004; Clay Robinson and Terry Kliewer, "Prairie View Students Can Register and Vote in Waller County, AG Rules," *Houston Chronicle*, February 5, 2004; Harvey Rice, "Prairie View Students Sue Again Over Voting," *Houston Chronicle*, February 18, 2004; Bruce Nichols, "Familiar Name Gets a New Script," *Dallas Morning News*, March 8, 2004; Terry Kliewer, "Waller County DA Apologizes in Vote Flap," *Houston Chronicle*, February 25, 2004; Terry Kliewer, "Students Head to Polls Early After Dispute," *Houston Chronicle*, February 26, 2004; Rhea Davis, "Embattled Waller County DA Will Step Down," August 28, 2004; Nichols, "Familiar Name Gets a New Script."

6. Samantha Sanchez, *Money and Diversity in State Legislatures 2003* (April 2005), 27–29, 36, 44, 50, 66, 69, 72; U.S. Census Bureau, "Table 4a. Reported Voting and Registration of the Total Voting-Age Population, by Sex, Race and Hispanic Origin, for States: November 2004," www.census.gov/population/socdemo/voting/cps2004/tab04a.xls; National League of Cities, "Demographic and Political Composition of City Councils," www.nlc.org/about_cities/cities_101/173.cfm; National League of Cities, "Number of Local Elected Officials," www.nlc.org/about_cities/cities_101/170.cfm; David A. Bositis, "Black Elected Officials: A Statistical Summary 2001," Joint Center for Political and Economic Studies, www.jointcenter.org/publication1/publication-PDFs/BEO-pdfs/2001-BEO.pdf; U.S. Senate, Senate State Information List, www.senate.gov/pagelayout/senators/f_two_sections_with_teasers/state.htm; U.S. Senate, Minorities in the Senate, www.senate.gov/artandhistory/history/common/briefing/minority_senators.htm; Ethnic Majority, African, Hispanic (Latino), and Asian American Members of Congress, www.ethnicmajority.com/congress.htm; State and Local Government on the Net, Governors and Lt. Governors, www.statelocalgov.net/50states-gov-ltgov.cfm; "Encyclopedia: List of United States Governors," www.nationmaster.com/encyclopedia/List-of-United-States-Governors.

7. Abigail M. Thernstrom, *Whose Votes Count? Affirmative Action and Minority Voting Rights* (Cambridge: Harvard University Press, 1987); Pamela S. Karlan and Peyton McCrary, "Without Fear and Without Research: Abigail Thernstrom on the Voting Rights Act," *Journal of Law and Politics* 4 (1988): 751–77; Bernard Grofman and Lisa Handley, "1990s Issues in Voting Rights," *Mississippi Law Journal* 65 (1995): 205, 233–34. States included in the calculation of citizens and elected officials are Alabama, Alaska, Arizona, Georgia, Louisiana, Mississippi, South Carolina, Texas, and Virginia. See Sanchez, *Money and Diversity in State Legislatures* 2003, 6, 9, 12, 15, 18, 27–76; U.S. Census Bureau, "Table 4a. Reported Voting and Registration."

8. Editorial, "Jackson's Plan Would Extend Voting Wrongs," *Mobile Register*, March 12, 2005; Samuel Issacharoff, "Is Section 5 of the Voting Rights Act a Victim of Its Own Success?" *Columbia Law Review* 105 (2004): 1731.

9. Deposition of Representative Phillip Steven King, November 23, 2003, *Session v. Perry*, United States District Court for the Eastern District of Texas, Marshall Division, 2:03-CV-00356: 82–85; Peyton McCrary, Christopher Seaman, Richard Valelly, "The End of Preclearance as We Knew It: How the Supreme Court Transformed Section 5 of the Voting Rights Act" (unpublished manuscript, 2005). The hypothetical regarding

the reapportionment committee chair who refused to draw a predominantly black district is based on the facts in the case of *Busbee v. Smith*, 549 F. Supp. 494 (D.D.C. 1982), *aff=d mem.*, 459 U.S. 1166 (1983), where the committee chair actually said, "I don't want to draw nigger districts."

10. Robert Behre, "County Might Settle $1.8M Voting Case," *Post and Courier* (Charleston, SC), February 11, 2004; Stephen Breyer, "Analyzing Regulatory Failure: Mismatches, Less Restrictive Alternatives, and Reform," *Harvard Law Review* 92 (1979): 547; Frances DeBerry, interview by Spencer Overton, July 25, 2005; Wayne Gilbert, interview by Spencer Overton, July 25, 2005; Robert Sheheen, interview by Spencer Overton, July 25, 2005.

11. Michael J. Pitts, "Let's Not Call the Whole Thing Off Just Yet: A Response to Samuel Issacharoff's Suggestion to Scuttle Section 5 of the Voting Rights Act," *Nebraska Law Review* 84 (forthcoming, 2005); *Enforcement of Voting Rights*, Public Law 91-285, codified at *U.S. Code* 42 (1970), sec. 1973c.

12. *South Carolina v. Katzenbach*, 383 U.S. 301, 359 (1966) (Black, J., dissenting).

13. *Lopez v. Monterey County*, 525 U.S. 266, 282 (1999).

14. Issacharoff, "Is Section 5 of the Voting Rights Act a Victim of its Own Success?": 1729; Editorial, "Jackson's Plan"; Civil Rights Division, U.S. Department of Justice, "Section 5 Covered Jurisdictions," www.usdoj.gov/crt/voting/sec_5/covered.htm (accessed July 28, 2005).

15. Chandler Davidson and Bernard Grofman, *Quiet Revolution in the South: The Impact of the Voting Rights Act 1965–1990* (Princeton, NJ: Princeton University Press, 1994), 378.

16. Gerry Hebert, e-mail message to author, August 1, 2005.

17. *Voting Rights Act of 1965*, sec. 4(a), sec. 4(f)(4).

18. Rachel S. Franklin, "Domestic Migration Across Regions, Divisions, and States: 1995 to 2000," *Census 2000 Special Reports* (August 2003), 2, www.census.gov/prod/2003pubs/censr-7.pdf.

19. National Conference of State Legislatures, "State Requirements for Voter Identification," www.legis.state.wi.us/lc/3_COMMITTEES/Special%20Committees/2004/ELAW/voterid_elaw.pdf (accessed June 27, 2005); see also National Conference of State Legislatures, "State Requirements for Voter Identification,"www.ncsl.org/programs/legman/elect/taskfc/voteridreq.htm (accessed June 27, 2005).

20. U.S. Department of Justice, Civil Rights Division, Litigation Brought by the Voting Section, www.usdoj.gov/crt/voting/litigation/caselist.htm; U.S. Department of Justice, Civil Rights Division, Section 5 Objection Determinations, www.usdoj.gov/crt/voting/sec_5/obj_activ.htm; U.S. Department of Justice, Civil Rights Division, About Federal Examiners and Federal Observers, www.usdoj.gov/crt/voting/examine/activ_exam.htm; U.S. Department of Justice, "Justice Department to Dispatch Federal Election Monitors to Alabama, California, and New Mexico," press release, June 1, 1998, www.usdoj.gov/opa/pr/1998/June/247cr.htm.html; U.S. Department of Justice, "Federal Observers and Justice Department Personnel to Monitor General Elections in States Across the Nation," press release, November 4, 2002, www.usdoj.gov/opa/pr/2002/November/02_crt_640.htm; U.S. Department of Justice, "Department of Justice Announces Federal Observers to Monitor General Election in States Across the Country," press release, October 28, 2004, www.usdoj.gov /opa/pr/2004/October/04_crt_725.htm; U.S. Census Bureau, "Table 4a. Reported Voting and Registration of the Total Voting-Age Population, by Sex, Race and Hispanic Origin, for States: November 2004," www.census.gov/population/socdemo/voting/cps2004/tab04a.xls; Ethnic Majority, African, Hispanic (Latino), and Asian American Members of Congress; State and Local Government on the Net; "Encyclopedia: List of United States Governors"; CNN.com, Election Results: U.S. President, www.cnn.com/ELECTION/2004/2004/pages/results/states/AL/P/00/epoll s.o.html (accessed on June 11, 2005); Michael Bocian, e-mail message to author, July 13, 2005; U.S. Census Bureau, "Reported Voting and Registration of the Total Voting-Age Population, by Sex, Race and Hispanic Origin, for States," www.census.gov/population/www/socdemo/voting/p20–542; U.S. Census Bureau, "Reported Voting and Registration of the Total Voting-Age Population, by Sex, Race and Hispanic Origin, for States," www.census.gov/population/www/socdemo/voting/past-voting.htm; U.S. Census Bureau, State and Country QuickFacts, http://quickfacts.census.gov/qfd; U.S. Department of Justice, "The Attorney General's Language Minority Guidelines: 28 C.F.R. Part 55: Appendix to Part 55— Jurisdictions Covered Under Section 203(c) of the Voting Rights Act of 1965, as Amended," www.usdoj.gov/crt/voting/28cfr/55/28cfr55.htm; FairData, Socio-Economic Contract Charts—Census 2000 Profiles, www.fairdata2000.com/SF3/contrast_charts/index.html.

21. Laughlin McDonald, "The Voting Rights Act in Indian Country: South Dakota, A Case Study," *American Indian Law Review* 29 (2004): 43; http://factfinder.census.gov/servlet/SAFFPeople?_sse=on.

Chapter Five

1. Colin Campbell, "Two Nights of Rioting Bring a Curfew to Lawrence, Mass.," *New York Times*, August 11, 1984; Bob Hohler, "5 years after riots, Lawrence's Hispanics Feel Betrayed, Angry," *Boston Globe*, August 13, 1989; Efrain Hernandez Jr., "Lawrence Schools Outnumbered," *Boston Globe*, September 12, 1990; Adrian Walker, "Mayor Mulls Resignation in Lawrence, Officials Say," *Boston Globe*, September 22, 1990; Jeremiah V. Murphy, "In Lawrence, Hispanics' Potential Untapped," *Boston Globe*, December 2, 1990; Diego Ribadeneira, "In Lawrence, Fears for Schools' Fate," *Boston Globe*, October 14, 1991; John Laidler, "Latinos in Lawrence Share Santiago Win," *Boston Globe*, October 4, 1998; Caroline Louise Cole, "Lawrence Hispanics Move into Politics," *Boston Globe*, October 7, 1997; United States Department of Justice, "Justice Department Sues Massachusetts City for Denying Hispanic Citizens Equal Participation in the Electoral Process," press release, November 5, 1998; Joe Heaney, "Feds Sue Lawrence for Bias vs. Hispanic Voters," *Boston Herald*, November 6, 1998; Jordana Hart, "Lawrence Vote Process Defended," *Boston Globe*, November 7, 1998; Tom Duggan, "The Racism Behind District School Committees," Paying Attention Webpage, July 1, 1999, www.tommyduggan.com/districts.html; United States Department of Justice, "Lawrence, Massachusetts to Settle Allegations of Voter Discrimination, Under Justice Department Agreement," press release, September 9, 1999; Ed Hayward, "Lawrence Agrees to Assist Hispanic Voters at Polls," *Boston Herald*, September 10, 1999; Mark E. Vogler, "New Majority Eyes a Seat at the Table," *Lawrence Eagle-Tribune*, August 10, 2001; Caroline Louise Cole, "Sullivan Tops Melendez in Closely Watched Race," *Boston Globe*, November 7, 2001; United States Department of Justice, "Voting Rights Settlement with Massachusetts City Will Increase Opportunities for Hispanic Voters to Elect Representatives of Their Choice," press release, February 25, 2002; Brian C. Mooney, "Mapping Latinos' Political Inroads—Good Old Politicking, Perseverance Pay Off," *Boston Globe*, October 16, 2002; Matthew T. Hall, "Recent Voting Probes Net Different Outcomes," *San Diego Union-Tribune*, July 19, 2003; "Short Circuits," *Boston Globe*, March 31, 1991; Aaron Zitner, "Democratic State Party Members Caucus for Open Committee Slot," *Boston Globe*, June 9, 1991.

2. Isabel Melendez, interview by Dan Taylor, July 31, 2005.

3. Garrine P. Laney, Congressional Research Service, *The Voting Rights Act of 1965, as Amended: Its History and Current Issues* (2004), 49–50;

"Voting Rights Act Amendments of 1992, Determinations Under Section 203," *Federal Register* 67 (July 26, 2002): 48,871; Tova Andrea Wang, "African Americans, Voting Machines, and Spoiled Ballots: A Challenge to Election Reform," The Century Foundation, September 14, 2004, www.tcf.org/Publications/ElectionReform/afamvoting.pdf (accessed May 10, 2005); Michael Waterstone, "Constitutional and Statutory Voting Rights for People with Disabilities," *Stanford Law & Policy Review* 14 (2003): 355; United States General Accounting Office, "Voters With Disabilities—Access to Polling Places and Alternative Voting Methods" (October 2001), 7, 32, www.gao.gov/new.items/d02107.pdf; Daniel P. Tokaji, "The Paperless Chase: Electronic Voting and Democratic Values," *Fordham Law Review* 73 (2005): 1744–47; *People of New York v. County of Schoharie*, 82 F.Supp. 2d 19 (2000). This book does not cover disability access to the voting process in greater depth because it is an exceptionally difficult and important subject that is worthy of a book in itself.

4. See Sylvia R. Lazos Vargas, "Deconstructing Homo[geneous] Americanus: The White Ethnic Immigrant Narrative and Its Exclusionary Effect," *Tulane Law Review* 72 (1998): 1493; Athena D. Mutua, "Shifting Bottoms and Rotating Centers: Reflections on LatCrit III and the Black/White Paradigm," *University of Miami Law Review* 53 (1999): 1177; U.S. English, Inc., www.us-english.org/inc/.

5. See Lazos Vargas, "Deconstructing Homo[geneous] Americanus": 1493; Mutua, "Shifting Bottoms and Rotating Centers": 1177; U.S. English, Inc., www.us-english.org/inc/; Senate Committee on the Judiciary, *Extension of the Voting Rights Act of 1965: Hearings on S. 407, S. 903, S. 1297, S. 1409 and S. 1443*, 94th Cong., 1st sess., 1975, 757; House Committee on the Judiciary, *Extension of the Voting Rights Act: Hearings Before the Subcommittee on Civil and Constitutional Rights of the House Committee on the Judiciary*, 97th Cong., 1st sess., 1981, 1001–5; Senate Committee on the Judiciary, *17 S. Hrg. 102-1066*, 102nd Cong., 2nd sess., 1992, 334; Juan F. Perea, "Demography and Distrust: An Essay on American Languages, Cultural Pluralism, and Official English," *Minnesota Law Review* 77 (1992): 274, 286; U.S. Census Bureau, Department of Commerce, "Hispanic and Asian Americans Increasing Faster Than Overall Population," June 14, 2004, www.census.gov/Press-Release/www/releases/archives/race/001839.html (accessed May 21, 2005); Office of Immigration Statistics, Department of Homeland Security, *2003 Yearbook of Immigration Statistics* (2003), 138–41; Bill Piatt, *¿Only English?: Law and Language Policy in the United States* (Albuquerque: University of New Mexico Press, 1990), 159; Paige Albinak, "NBC's Other Language," *Broadcasting and Cable*, January 3, 2005.

6. Robert Klein Engler, "The Need to Repeal Section 203 of the Voting Rights Act," ChronWatch, News & Editorials, September 17, 2004, www.chronwatch.com/content/contentDisplay.asp?aid=9755 (accessed June 28, 2005); November 2, 2004, Ballot, Alachua County, Florida, "Proposed Constitutional Amendment, No. 3 Constitutional Amendment Article I, Section 26," http://elections.alachua.fl.us/images/Ballots/E.pdf (accessed June 2, 2005); Rodolfo O. de la Garza and Louis DeSipio, "Save the Baby, Change the Bathwater, and Scrub the Tub: Latino Electoral Participation After Seventeen Years of Voting Rights Act Coverage," *Texas Law Review* 71 (1993): 1518; Frank M. Lowrey IV, "Comment, Through the Looking Glass: Linguistic Separatism and National Unity," *Emory Law Journal* 41 (1992): 265–86; U.S. Citizenship and Immigration Services, Department of Homeland Security, "General Naturalization Requirements," http://uscis.gov/graphics/services/natz/general.thm (accessed May 11, 2005); *U.S. Code* 8 (2004), sec. 1423; U.S. Census Bureau, Department of Commerce, "Language Spoken at Home for the Citizen Population 18 Years and Over Who Speak English Less Than English 'Very Well,' for the United States, States, and Counties: 2000," www.census.gov/mp/www/spectab/languagespokenSTP194.xls (accessed May 20, 2005); U.S. Census Bureau, Department of Commerce, "Profile of the Foreign-Born Population in the United States: 2000," www.census.gov/prod/2002pubs/p23-206.pdf (accessed May 20, 2005); de la Garza and DeSipio, "Save the Baby, Change the Bathwater": 1536–39 (see tables 11 and 12 regarding bilingual-ballot usage from data collected through the Latino National Political Survey [LNPS]). Note that only Latinos who responded to the Spanish version of the survey (rather than the English version) were asked the bilingual-ballot questions, and that the low number of respondents (only 167 individuals polled in Spanish replied that bilingual materials were available when they voted) may have increased the risk of error. Asian American Legal Defense and Education Fund, *The Asian-American Vote: A Report on the AALDEF Multilingual Exit Poll in the 2004 Presidential Election* (2005), 2; www.census.gov/Press-Release/www/releases/archives/CB05-73Table1.xls.

7. De la Garza and Louis DeSipio, "Save the Baby, Change the Bathwater": 1482–83; United States Department of Justice, "Ensuring Compliance with the Language Minority Provisions of the Voting Rights Act," http://usinfo.state.gov/usa/civilrights/fs072303.htm; "Voting Rights Act Amendments of 1992, Determinations Under Section 203," *Federal Register* 67 (July 26, 2002): 48,871; Glenn D. Magpantay, "Asian American Access to the Vote: The Language Assistance Provisions (Section 203) of the Voting Rights Act and Beyond," *Asian Law Journal* 11 (2004): 31;

Caroline J. Tolbert and Rodney E. Hero, "Dealing with Diversity: Racial/Ethnic Context and Social Policy Change," *Political Research Quarterly* 54 (2001): 571; Peter Harris and Ben Reilly, eds., International Institute for Democracy and Electoral Assistance, Democracy and Deep-Rooted Conflict: Options for Negotiators, 1998, available at www.int-idea.se/publications/democracy_and_deep_rooted_conflict/upload/ddrc_full_en.pdf; Michael DeChiara, Note, "A Modern Day Myth: The Necessity of English as the Official Language," *Boston College Third World Law Journal* 17: 101, 105–6 (1997); Geoffrey Nunberg, "Linguists and the Official Language Movement," *Language* 65 (1989): 579, 580; Sandra Guerra, "Voting Rights and the Constitution: The Disenfranchisement of Non-English Speaking Citizens," *Yale Law Journal* 97 (1988): 1419; Kathryn A. Woolard, "Sentences in the Language Prison: The Rhetorical Structuring of an American Language Policy Debate," *American Ethnologist* 16 (1989): 268; Chalsa M. Loo, "The 'Biliterate' Ballot Controversy: Language Acquisition and Cultural Shift Among Immigrants," *International Migration Review* 19 (1985): 493.

8. Rita Taylor, Town Clerk, Briny Breezes, Florida, telephone interview with Dan Taylor, August 1, 2005; George Bennett, "Ballots Set for 18 Local Elections," *Palm Beach Post,* February 9, 2005, 1B; Fred Alvarez, "Stepping Up for Bilingual Voters," *Los Angeles Times*, October 27, 2004; Michael Browning, "Living In (and Out of) a Can," *Palm Beach Post,* August 22, 2004, 1D; United States General Accounting Office, *Bilingual Voting Assistance: Assistance Provided and Costs* (May 1997), 20–21. The estimated cost per voter is based on the assumption that about 200,000 polling places exist in the United States and each polling place, on average, serves about 607 voters. James Tucker and Rodolfo Espino, Minority Language Assistance Study (2005); Congressional Budget Office, "Analysis of the Effects on State and Local Governments of H.R. 3295, *The Martin Luther King Jr. Voting Rights Act of 2001*, as Passed by the Senate," September 27, 2002, www.cbo.gov/ftpdocs/38xx/doc3842/S565_SL.pdf (accessed June 28, 2005); CNN.com, "Election Results: U.S. President," www.cnn.com/ELECTION/2004/pages/results/president/ (accessed June 28, 2005); General Accounting Office, *Bilingual Voting Assistance*: 3, 10–11; Tokaji, "The Paperless Chase": 1747–48; "U.S. Citizenship/Naturalization: Interview Questions & Answers (100)," www.vkblaw.com/law/natzq.htm#important_right (accessed June 28, 2005).

9. Fiona Yung, "Chinatown Ballot Shows 'Republican' as 'Democrat,'" *Village Voice*, November 15, 2000, www.villagevoice.com/news/0046, yung,19793,5.html (accessed May 11, 2005); General Accounting Office, *Bilingual Voting Assistance*: 2; Engler, "The Need to Repeal Section 203

of the Voting Rights Act"; English First Foundation, "Bilingual Ballots: Election Fairness or Fraud?" www.englishfirst.org/eff/efbb.htm; Jim Boulet, Jr., "Bilingual Chaos: Another Election Scandal," www.english first.org/ballots/nrballots121900.htm; Jonathan N. Wand et al., "The Butterfly Did It: The Aberrant Vote for Buchanan in Palm Beach County, Florida," *American Political Science Review* 95 (2001): 793; Voter Verification in the Federal Elections Process: Hearing Before the Sen. Rules and Admin. Comm., 109th Cong. (2005); Jenny Marder, "Cure Available for Ballot Confusion," *Tri-Valley Herald* (Pleasanton, CA), October 26, 2004.

Chapter Six

1. Terry Woster, "S.D. Tribes Question Photo ID Voter Law," *Sioux Falls* [SD] *Argus Leader*, July 16, 2004; Denise Ross, "Voter I.D. Law Merits, Flaws Debated," *Rapid City* [SD] *Journal,* July 16, 2004; Chet Brokaw, "Lawmakers Asked to Repeal Voter Identification Law," *Aberdeen* [SD] *News*, July 15, 2004; Adam Cohen, "Indians Face Obstacles Between the Reservation and the Ballot Box," *New York Times*, June 21, 2004; Laughlin McDonald, "The Voting Rights Act in Indian Country: South Dakota, a Case Study," *American Indian Law Review* 29 (2004–2005).

2. John Mark Hansen, "Report Issued by the Task Force on the Federal Election System" July 2001, www.reformelections.org/ncfer.asp; see also Michelle Waslin, "Safe Roads, Safe Communities: Immigrants and State Driver's License Requirements" (May 2002), National Council of La Raza, www.nclr.org/policy/briefs/IB6Drivers%20License.pdf (accessed June 28, 2005); Deval L. Patrick, Assistant Attorney General, Civil Rights Division of the U.S. Department of Justice, to Sheri Morris, Assistant Attorney General for the State of Louisiana, November 21, 1994; Brokaw, "Lawmakers Asked to Repeal Voter Identification Law"; Gabrielle B. Ruda, "Note, Picture Perfect: A Critical Analysis of the Debate on the 2002 Help America Vote Act," *Fordham Urban Law Journal* 31 (2003): 240; Hansen, "Report Issued by the Task Force on the Federal Election System," 4.

3. 42 U.S.C. § 1973i(c), Lorraine Minnite and David Callahan, *Securing the Vote: An Analysis of Election Fraud* (2003), available at www.demos.org/pubs/EDR_-_Securing_the_Vote.pdf; Coalition on Homelessness and Housing in Ohio and League of Women Voters Coalition, *Let the People Vote* (2005), available at www.cohhio.org/alerts/Election%20Reform%20 Report.pdf; letter from Cathy Cox, Georgia Secretary of State, to Sonny Perdue, Georgia Governor, April 8, 2005, available at www.aclu.org/Files/

OpenFile.cfm?id=18651; *Borders v. King County,* No. 05-2-00027-3, Washington Superior Court, Chelan County, June 24, 2005, available at www.secstate.wa.gov/documentvault/694.pdf; Gregory Roberts, "Six More Charged With Offenses in 2004 Election," *Seattle Post-Intelligencer,* June 22, 2005, at B1; 42 U.S.C. § 15483(a)(2)(A)(ii); The Brennan Center for Justice and Spencer Overton, *Response to the Report of the 2005 Commission on Federal Election Reform* (2005), available at www.carter bakerdissent.com.

4. Louis Massicotte, André Blais, and Antoine Yoshinaka, *Establishing the Rules of the Game: Election Laws in Democracies,* 2004.

5. Rob Randhava, "Fears of Vote Suppression Beginning to Materialize," The Progressive Coalition for Equal Opportunity and Justice, November 5, 2002, www.civil rights.org/issues/voting/details.cfm?id=10540; Lori Minnite and David Callahan, *Demos, Securing the Vote: An Analysis of Election Fraud* (2003), 30; The Citywide Coalition for Voter Participation, "Groups Protest Senate Bill for Voter ID Checks; Say Will Make Many New Yorkers 'Second Class Voters,' " news release, April 3, 2002; "Hispanic Right to Vote Challenged," October 26, 2004, www.walb.com/ Global/story.asp?S=2484078&nav=5kZQSQlS (accessed June 28, 2005); John Nolan, "Felons Have Problems in Getting Right to Vote Restored," Associated Press, August 20, 2004; Robert A. Pastor, "Improving the U.S. Electoral System: Lessons from Canada and Mexico," *Election Law Journal* 3 (2004), 584.

Conclusion

1. Michael Waterstone, "Constitutional and Statutory Voting Rights for People with Disabilities," *Stanford Law & Policy Review* 14 (2003): 364; Lani Guinier, *The Tyranny of the Majority: Fundamental Fairness in Representative Democracy* (New York: Free Press, 1994), 93; Guy-Uriel E. Charles, "Racial Identity, Electoral Structures, and the First Amendment Right of Association," *California Law Review* 91 (2003); Pamela S. Karlan, "Politics by Other Means," *Virginia Law Review* 85 (1999); Alec C. Ewald, American Voting: The Local Character of Suffrage in the United States (unpublished dissertation, February 2005); Kristin L. Adair, "Keeping Up Appearances: The Role of Partisan Politics in U.S. Election Administration and the Need for Reform" (unpublished manuscript, 2005); Pamela S. Karlan, "The Rights to Vote: Some Pessimism About Formalism," *Texas Law Review* 71 (1993): 1705; Heather K. Gerken, "Understanding the Right to an Undiluted Vote," *Harvard Law Review* 114 (2001): 1663.

2. Thom Hartmann, *What Would Jefferson Do?* (New York: Random House/Harmony, 2004), 256.

3. Nan Morehead (board member, Common Cause Colorado), in telephone interview by Meredith Sharoky, June 22, 2005; Jack Gould (issue chair, Common Cause Nebraska), in telephone interview by Meredith Sharoky, June 18, 2005; Jack Taylor (state chair, Common Cause New Mexico), in telephone interview by Meredith Sharoky, June 18, 2005; Odetta MacLeish-White (board member, National League of Women Voters), in telephone interview by Meredith Sharoky, July 2005; Kay J. Maxwell (president, National League of Women Voters), in telephone interview by Meredith Sharoky, July 2, 2005; Judith Palafox Rodriguez (Ventura County Board of Elections), in telephone interview by Meredith Sharoky, June 2005; Clarissa Martinez De Castro (director of state public policy for the National Council of La Raza), in telephone interview by Meredith Sharoky, August 1, 2005; Marcie Graham (president of NYU NAACP chapter), in telephone interview by Meredith Sharoky, July 27, 2005.

INDEX